食品愈合

Urban Remedy

Neka Pasquale, M.S., L.Ac.

photographs by
Thayer Allyson Gowdy

weldon**owen**

DEDICATION & ACKNOWLEDGMENTS

I want to begin by thanking my parents, who exposed me to the true farm-to-table experience living off the land in the Humboldt mountains during their hippie years. Both of you have been amazing examples of living life to the sound of your own drum—mom creating a successful business based on health, healing, and beauty, and dad living life as a true artist, seeker, traveler, veteran, amazing cook, writer, and builder. You both have inspired me in your own ways and given me the tools to start and run my own business while fully expressing my creativity.

I also want to thank all of the patients that I have treated over the ten-plus years in my Acupuncture practice. You showed me that the most important aspects of healing are to listen and acknowledge your pain, pleasure, defeats, and wins. You help me remember that the bottom line to all healing is love. Being witness to the power of Chinese medicine has changed who I am and how I think and I am forever in awe of this ancient art. I am eternally grateful for all the teachers along the way. Dr. Robert Marshall, you are a pioneer, an inspiration, and one of the smartest guys I've ever met. George Conley, you take healing to a whole other level. Thank you for your work and dedication to your craft. I am also grateful to Barbara Custer for taking all my patients after I closed my practice and keeping me balanced during my challenges and changes. Finally, Kersten Marie, my friend and healer, you are the real deal and I love you.

I want to thank Jamie Shaw, without whom I could not have completed this project. I love sharing our foodie moments while sipping roasted dandelion tea. You "got" me from the beginning and have always helped me express myself. You are smart as a whip and you know what I'm saying before I can end the sentence, which says it all. Thank you!

Thanks to Sally Ekus, my agent who helped me find the perfect home for this book at Weldon Owen. Jennifer Newens and Amy Marr, thank you for believing in this project and making it happen. Your insights have been invaluable and your kindness deeply appreciated. Thayer Gowdy, thank you for helping to realize my aesthetic vision with your beautiful imagery and ability to make me laugh and smile. I owe you a raw lasagne! To all the stylists and the creative team, you are the best.

I am so grateful to Cindy Crawford for believing in me and helping me shine a light on this knowledge to empower others for optimal health. Thank you for joining me on this journey—you are an inspiration.

My Urban Remedy family: I am so grateful for all of your support and belief in my vision, especially my earliest supporters, The Science Inc. team, Marcelo, and the UR Brazilian beauties, Juliana, Roberta, and Alejandro. Ushi Patel, you crafted the heart and soul of Urban Remedy and helped make my dreams come true. Rachel and Jody, thank you both for your mad styling skills and friendship. And Mandypants, thanks for helping me all along the way, from our teeny, tiny shared kitchen to today and everything in between: babies, marriage, divorce. We need a vacation!

Heartfelt thanks to my BFF, Paul Stukin, for always believing in me (just please stop stealing my recipes). And much gratitude to the other angels in my life: Rach, Simmone, Nicole, Desi, Dana, Gina, Molly, Anna OD, John Wigmore, Sanna my fairy Godmother, and Suzie!

This book is dedicated to my angels in heaven: my Grandmother Ruth for her unconditional love and wild spirit and my father Frank Pasquale, a true one-of-a-kind man. I love and miss you both every day. And to my wildly alive son, Frankie Love. Sharing life with you is pure joy and my love for you is limitless.

FOREWORD

I met Neka through a mutual friend who knows I'm always interested in finding new ways to use food to enrich and support my lifestyle. I was quickly impressed with her knowledge, her background in traditional Chinese medicine, and her passion for healing with food—not to mention the delicious recipes she creates—so we connected immediately. Today, she is my go-to resource for nutrition. I love that her approach is about health and life and enjoyment, not deprivation.

Like many people, I had heard plenty about juicing, fasting, and cleansing, but when I walked up to a juice bar, I felt overwhelmed with the choices offered, based on the often contradictory information out there. Do the ingredients always have to be organic or not? Should I worry about the high sugar content of many of the juices? How do I know which juice is the best one for me?

With Neka, I was happy to have a trusted voice to advise me about different ingredients and their associated health benefits. What I have learned from her has empowered me to make better-informed decisions. Whether it's a four-day cleanse, a single day of clean eating, or a particular recipe to treat a common ailment,

I look to Neka for delicious, healing recipes that will help me feel my best.

Even if I'm not cleansing, I like to have a protein meal–replacement smoothie in the morning. I can drink it while I take my kids to school and then I have the energy for my workout. I also try to drink at least one green drink a day, so I'm sure to get all the benefits and antioxidants that leafy green vegetables offer. With Neka's guidance, I have passed along healing recommendations that have helped my sister, and, amazingly, my husband has become a kale salad lover!

Today, my passion is helping to shine a light on people doing great work, so I'm thrilled to recommend Neka's cleanse, as well as her general expertise and recipes. If I can use my voice to help more people discover the benefits I've enjoyed from Urban Remedy, I'm happy to do it. I know you're going to love the powerful knowledge and delicious creations that Neka shares—and that you're going to feel fantastic once you have put them to work in your own life!

To health and happiness,

Welcome to Urban Remedy

Over the course of my career as a nutritional consultant and acupuncturist, I have bridged my passion for health, cooking, and healing with an understanding of how to use food as medicine. And because I was raised in a health-conscious family, have practiced traditional Chinese medicine for over a decade, and live in the farm-to-table culture of Northern California, I've always been surrounded by people who care about what they eat and who strive to eat for health as well as pleasure.

All of those factors led me to found Urban Remedy, a company that sells fresh, raw, cold-pressed organic juices and raw vegan snacks and other foods, in 2009. I started the company as a way to share with people the incredible benefits natural ingredients offer in preventing and curing so many common ailments. But even before that, I was making juices for 4- to 7-day retreats that I was leading—healing getaways designed to remove people from their regular routines and habits, with the goal of rebooting mind, body, and spirit. What I observed on these retreats surpassed even my greatest expectations of what people might achieve in a short amount of time. Over and over again, participants described feeling transformative results by resetting body and mind over the course of just a few days.

I wrote this book because I want to share the potent experience of a healing retreat with as many people as possible. Through my self-guided program, you can enjoy the same powerful and pampering benefits as my clients here in Northern California do—all in the comfort of your home and without the cost of travel or lodging.

WHAT IS A CLEANSE?

A cleanse is a gift you give yourself. It's a conscious decision to examine every aspect of your life and take active steps to reset and revitalize. It's a chance to embrace healthy new habits and leave the bad ones behind. Urban Remedy retreats are a labor of love for me—a chance to share my knowledge of Chinese medicine and acupuncture, superfoods, cold-pressed juices, meditation, yoga, and delicious recipes. I have always loved the idea of dedicating time to better health and self-improvement, and now, with this book, I've found a way to help you do that in your own home, possibly with friends if you choose to make it a group experience. As a practitioner of Chinese medicine, I am a firm believer in balance. So my retreats are designed to cleanse every aspect of your being. The Eastern system of medicine teaches that, in order to achieve optimal health, you must treat mind, body, and spirit equally. That is to say, you can eat a healthy diet, but if you are living in emotional turmoil or heavy stress, your body will suffer. Likewise, you can meditate and do yoga every day to control your stress, but if you eat a solid diet of junk food, you'll still be out of balance. Your Urban Remedy cleanse retreat will teach you how to address all aspects of your health in the course of a four-day detox program designed to impart skills that you can use for life.

Why do we need to detox?

The typical American diet is not a healthy one. For years, we have been told to eat a low-fat diet and stay away from saturated fats and eat foods high in polyunsaturated fats and carbohydrates. Americans have been following these guidelines and yet, we are sicker than ever. New studies show that this diet supports chronic inflammation, which is the precursor to diabetes, heart disease, stroke, and obesity. When we consistently eat foods that promote inflammation, like white flour, white sugar, white rice, French fries, high-fructose corn syrup, omega-6 oils (soybean, corn and sunflower oils); foods with preservatives; and sugar-rich beverages like sodas and highly sweetened coffee drinks, we are promoting unhealthy inflammation in our bodies.

A better way to eat is to consume foods as close to their natural state as possible like fresh organic fruits and nuts; superfoods like cacao, hemp, goji berries, and chia; healthy fats and powerful spices like coconut oil, turmeric, garlic, and ginger; and vibrantly colored vegetables that contain antioxidants that stamp out inflammatory free radicals. Instead of hormone-laden eggs and meats choose pastured and grass-fed (these foods are not only better for you, but also better for the environment).

It is important to cleanse because many health problems today are caused by the buildup of toxic waste in the body. We take in toxins from our environment by inhaling them, ingesting them, or coming into physical contact with them. Drugs, food additives, and allergens can build harmful toxins in the body. Our bodies also produce toxins internally through biochemical and cellular functions, which generate substances that need to be eliminated. When these toxins aren't eliminated, they can cause irritation or inflammation of the cells and tissues, blocking normal functions on a cellular, organ, and whole-body level, all of which can lead to disease. (Some people's systems tend to have poor detoxifying powers and need nutritional support. Ingredients that can help open these detoxification pathways are vitamins B12 and B6, vitamin C, turmeric, and milk thistle). But environmental toxins aren't the only culprits. Our negative thoughts, emotions, and stress also generate toxicity—something I will talk more about when I review the principles of traditional Chinese medicine in the next chapter. Eradication of this emotional toxicity is just as essential as ridding the body of environmental toxins.

Toward that end, I have designed my retreats to help participants cleanse themselves of emotional or spiritual baggage—think toxic habits, crippling relationships, and stagnant routines. Detoxification is a transformational medicine that creates change on many levels. Cleansing the body while intentionally, mindfully examining our emotional toxicity helps us release lingering problems from our past. We are forced to break out of bad habits and needless distractions in order to focus on what truly matters and reset our routines and intentions. When our bodies eliminate toxic buildup—both environmental and emotional— we feel lighter and less burdened, so we can more fully experience the moment, set goals, and become open to a better future.

You'll be amazed to see the kinds of epiphanies and life changes that can come out of a retreat— to see how just a few days of self-care and

inward examination can be a catalyst for change and improvement. I am always stunned by the transformations I witness in this setting—small ones and staggering ones—and that aspect of the program has always driven me forward. This is work that I enjoy. I am committed to a life of healing, and knowing that I can help people treat themselves by using food as medicine is the greatest reward possible.

Can I really do a retreat at home?

Yes, you can. And it will be virtually the same as the retreats I lead for my clients. Sure, you will have to prepare the food yourself, but I'll give you all of the tools and lessons you need to keep the food simple and delicious. That said, this cleanse is designed for food lovers. You're going to be in the kitchen. You're going to be making things, and doing that is going to take time and energy. But the experience is rewarding. The mindful work is part of the process, and the results—a clearer mind, lighter body, improved outlook—are worth it.

If I could, I would lead retreats every day of the year. But retreats are, by their very nature, expensive for some people, plus taking four days away from work or home can be difficult. I know what a powerful gift a retreat can be, however, and because I want to share it with as many people as I can reach, I've created this program to guide you remotely just as I would in person. One of the best things about a home retreat is that it is affordable and doable for anyone committed to putting in some time and energy to make it happen. I guarantee you'll spend less on food than you would in a normal week, and you'll be eating the freshest, most natural ingredients in truly satisfying preparations.

While other health programs might feel like a kind of punishment through deprivation, my home retreat is designed to pamper and nourish you. I want you to feel like you're spending a week at a luxury spa. I am going to teach you how to make spa-quality recipes and practice spa techniques for relaxation and revitalization. I'll also share pampering how-to guides, spa baths for detox and relaxation, and rituals that give you a tangible way to make a conscious break with spiritual baggage, pain, and bad habits. Did I mention that I used to co-own a spa with my mother at which I practiced acupuncture? That's where I learned a lot of wonderful techniques for relaxation and rejuvenation.

Coupled with my knowledge of ancient healing practices and modern, cutting-edge nutrition, my cleanse is a powerful program that sets the stage for you to discover your most radiant self and create lasting change. Don't get me wrong: You'll be doing challenging work on your retreat. But there's no reason it cannot be fun and restorative at the same time. Indeed, that's when a retreat works best.

This at-home retreat is more than a health program. It's not specifically designed with one goal in mind, like weight loss or antiaging or treating a health condition, though it just may do all those things. The reality is, this work carries with it all sorts of health benefits: you'll lower inflammation; alkalinize your body's pH; and get a jump start on a healthier lifestyle. After taking part in my cleanse, you'll feel at the height of your vitality and you'll be inspired to rethink your daily habits.

In addition to learning how to do a 4-day cleanse, you'll also learn about foods that work for your particular constitution or ailments based on the tenets of traditional Chinese medicine. You'll discover what foods to cut and what foods or ingredients have healing properties you can use. You'll be armed with scores of healthful and delicious recipes. Plus, you'll discover powerful new ways to release stress and dump emotional baggage.

What can I expect on my cleanse retreat?

Every day, you'll treat yourself to fresh juices and natural foods. Trust me when I say that I'm a foodie first and that I don't make anything that doesn't taste great (with the exception of maybe one particular bitter green juice, which I have learned to love). So I'm delighted to share my favorite recipes and shopping and preparation tips. I'll suggest some easy-to-adopt activities, and I'll teach you some powerful rituals for cleansing yourself of negative patterns and emotions. Sometimes having a ritual around the idea of letting negative thoughts and actions go makes it more real and easier to act on.

I've also found ways to make your cleanse as hands-on or as convenient as you want it to be. You can choose to make all of the juices and foods yourself, or, to save time and energy, you can order them from my website, *urbanremedy.com*. Although I fully encourage doing it yourself so you learn healthy habits and preparations, I know that changing dietary patterns and adopting new habits all at once can be overwhelming, especially when it means foregoing comforting foods and routines. Or, it may be that you cannot take time off from work, or make time to prepare your own meals. If you fit any of these circumstances, ordering from the website may be the best solution.

What results should I expect?

Routinely, after doing my cleanse, people tell me that they feel better than ever, mentally as well as physically. And that's not surprising after four days of clean food, rest, relaxation, and focus. Also, the simple act of devoting yourself to your own self-care has powerful resonance. It's empowering to know that you committed to a program just for you, and that you made the decision to become your best self. I have been lucky to witness radical changes in many of my guests after just a single retreat.

MICHAEL The moment Michael arrived at the retreat, he noticed the space was buzzing with inspiration and openness, an environment that immediately gave him a sense of positivity. He had been feeling stuck for several years and was seeking change. Through the retreat, Michael found the vision and the guidance he needed. He had little experience with eating raw foods and was surprised by the wide range of flavors and the satisfaction he experienced at each meal. The "in-between meal" juices were also a first for him, and he found them both delicious and filling. The new diet, coupled with meditation, yoga, hikes, group support, acupuncture, and infrared saunas, proved a recipe for success. After leaving the retreat, Michael felt cleansed on many levels. He continued to practice what he had learned during his stay. Within 6 months, he had lost 35 pounds (17 kg), and he has maintained that healthy weight. He has also developed a greater awareness around choosing healthy foods, exercising, meditation, and has a complete sense of well-being—all because of the retreat. Now, some 6½ years later, he continues to live a healthy and vital life.

VALERIE Valerie joined a retreat when she was going through an especially difficult time. She was in the middle of a divorce and had three small children, one of them recently adopted from Russia. When her husband left her, Valerie felt unable to cope. She was exhausted, overwhelmed, and had no energy. She felt helpless to continue. The retreat turned things around for her. By taking four days for herself, during which she ate healthy foods and focused on her life, Valerie was able to find the clarity she needed to make hard decisions. After rough patches in the past, she had always taken her husband back. Now, newly empowered with a view toward self-care, she knew she had to fight to do the right thing for herself. She learned how to convert raw foods into elegant meals, make her own nut milks, create delicious desserts for her kids, and integrate wheatgrass and superfoods like açai into her regular regimen— all of which gave her the sense of a new lease on life. Over the next few months, Valerie had a new set of tools that served as a metaphor for the emotional tools she was developing. She lost nearly ten pounds and felt strong and energetic again, truly able to care for herself and her children. Her emotional state had been making her feel dull and heavy, with poor digestion, and the retreat had helped her bounce back, both physically and emotionally.

ROSE It was apparent when she arrived that Rose had a lot of health issues. You could see in her demeanor that she was stressed; frankly, she was unpleasant. Rose described bodily pain and aches as well as depleted energy— probably the wide-ranging symptoms that we call fibromyalgia. Rose had been in pain for twenty years, and was accustomed to her unhappiness. She ate a diet primarily consisting of refined flour, sugar, and processed foods (which, unfortunately, is all too common in the American diet). She couldn't be active and was not energetic, and it seemed to me that she was trying to eat away her pain. Because her body wasn't vital, Rose was depressed. I must admit that upon meeting her, I thought it would be difficult to have Rose on the retreat. I worked hard to develop a positive, nurturing program and I didn't know how she'd react. But what happened over our five days together felt miraculous. She came out of the retreat like a new person. At the end of our time together, Rose reported that 80 percent of her pain was gone. She had lost weight and looked forward to this new phase of her life. I believe deeply that the program and diet that Rose followed during the retreat had the power to start her healing process, but I also feel strongly that taking the time to focus on and nurture herself had powerful effects on her mental and emotional state. When Rose left the retreat, she employed a whole new approach to eating and she credits this retreat with kickstarting a healthy lifestyle.

How is Urban Remedy different from other cleanse programs?

1. The program features a holistic point of view. My background in traditional Chinese medicine allows me to apply centuries-old principles of using food to heal ailments, which I combine with cutting-edge nutritional practices. Through my program, you'll learn to make food that increases your energy, promotes optimal health, and tastes amazing. More than that, you'll create a home retreat, which is a comprehensive and holistic way to care for mind, body, and spirit. You'll get all the secrets to guiding your own cleanse, and you'll be empowered with tools you can use to change your bad habits and patterns—your whole lifestyle, really—for good.

2. You'll actually eat well. My cleansing program is designed for people who adore food. You'll notice that my juices and dishes don't taste like health food. Instead, they are vibrant and flavorful, spiced or sweetened to perfection. The recipes are designed for maximum enjoyment, right down to textural combinations and pleasing presentations. Through the course of the cleanse, you will taste the difference and discover combinations you'll both savor and crave.

3. You will pamper yourself. Plenty of books tell you what to cut out, but few tell you what to add to your life in the way of not only nutrition and supplements but also habits, treatments, and rituals that will restore you, build you up, and give you the confidence and reassurance to make big changes.

4. You can customize your cleanse to meet your specific needs. This book includes information for most common ailments, both simple and serious. If you have acid reflux, I'll be advising you to eat more cabbage. If you are prediabetic, you should avoid fruit juice and adopt a low-glycemic diet in order to cut back on natural sweetness that spikes your blood sugar. There are countless ways that food can be applied to treat specific conditions, andI'll be sharing a wealth of that powerful information throughout.

What happens on a typical day?

Although you'll be easing up on your usual food intake and slowing down physically, cleanse days are surprisingly full and enriching. Time that might ordinarily be spent rushing around, carpooling kids, attending meetings, or cleaning house is going to be reserved for tending to yourself in ways that require a different kind of mindful, calming energy. I find the tasks associated with preparing a cleanse meditative and reflective, not to mention rewarding. You'll be preparing foods, examining and writing about your goals, getting outside to exercise, and pampering yourself with baths and rituals. We so rarely carve out time to take care of ourselves, and doing it for four consecutive days is a good way to remind yourself what self-care feels like. Giving yourself permission to pamper yourself in this way will reignite your ambition to make time for some of these moments within your regular routine. The complete cleanse activities are outlined on pages 56–99. You can add in a variety of supplementary activities, from yoga or saunas to massage and colonics, and I detail them on pages 97–99.

It doesn't matter if you're new to cleansing or consider yourself a cleansing veteran. I'll start with information about how to prepare yourself before the cleanse by removing all inflammatory foods, alcohol, sugar, white flour, meat, dairy, processed foods, and carbonated soda. At the same time, you'll be learning how to release all inflammatory or negative thought patterns that can hold you back from discovering your natural radiance. Over the course of four days, you'll be letting go of anything and everything that is promoting negativity or disease (read: dis-ease) in your body, mind, and spirit.

WHAT IS TRADITIONAL CHINESE MEDICINE?

Traditional Chinese medicine (TCM) is a centuries-old medical practice that looks at the root causes of symptoms and ailments and attempts to balance those causes, rather than treating symptoms. Through a complex understanding of the energy and balance in the body, and a profound knowledge of the healing properties of potent natural ingredients, practitioners of TCM use diet as a healing tool to prevent and treat disease, coupling it with acupuncture and other practices to stimulate energetic movement and restore balance in the body. The following brief overview of the philosophy and practices of TCM is designed to help you understand the tradition and thinking behind the work I do and how it applies to a cleanse and to the idea of using food as medicine.

The mind-body connection

One of the central tenets of TCM is that the mind, body, and spirit are all connected. So if one area of your being is weak or in pain, it can manifest as an imbalance in another system. As a professional practitioner of TCM, I've learned how bodily symptoms and pain can be correlated to specific emotions and imbalances. The easiest way to think about this concept is through this common example: many of my acupuncture patients with lower back pain revealed that they felt unsupported in their lives, be it at work, in a relationship, or with family. So the physical lack of support they experienced—in their back or spine—mirrored an emotional deficit in their lives. That symbolism is a potent part of Eastern medicine, and one that I embrace, as it has been relevant to many of my clients with many different conditions over the years. Because understanding this connection has become the primary tool in my healing practice, it is important that you grasp how TCM classifies the connections between certain emotions and specific organs. This will also be helpful as you evaluate your own physical state of balance.

The five elements

The five-element system represents the interconnectedness of the seasons, our organ system, emotions, climates, color, sound, and so on. These elements represent how we are connected to one another, the environment, and the natural order of life.

According to Chinese tradition, winter is associated with water, cold climate, salty taste, the emotion fear, and the organ kidney. When it starts to get colder, we naturally slow down and become more inward and take time or reflection. It's the time of year animals hibernate and nature becomes still. Because it is a time of stillness, we must take heed and not become stagnant. Going inward and looking at our fears,

FIVE ELEMENT CORRESPONDENCES IN TCM

	WOOD	FIRE	EARTH	METAL	WATER
ORGANS	Liver Gallbladder	Heart Small Intestine	Spleen Stomach	Lungs Large intestines	Kidney Bladder
SEASON	Spring	Summer	Late Summer	Fall	Winter
TASTE	Sour	Bitter	Sweet	Pungent	Salty
COLOR	Green	Red	Yellow	White	Dark blue-black
EMOTION	Anger	Joy	Worry	Sadness	Fear
CLIMATE FACTOR	Wind	Heat	Humidity	Dryness	Cold
MENTAL ATTRIBUTES	Rationality	Spirituality	Tranquility	Sentimentality	Desire

we can learn and grow. The ideas planted during winter can manifest and sprout into reality once spring arrives. Give yourself plenty of warm nourishment incorporating warm herbal teas and soups. Once springtime arrives, we've had enough rest and reflection to let the seeds of change we planted during the winter months germinate and grow with the new sunlight and warmth of the spring.

Spring is related to the liver and gallbladder so it is the best time to do a deep cleanse. The emotion associated with spring is anger, the color is green, the taste is sour, and the element is wood. Each season represents how to live in harmony with our surroundings and following these cycles keeps us balanced and in harmony.

Looking at a cleanse from a TCM perspective

As I've mentioned, the idea behind a cleanse is to give your mind, body, and spirit a break and some much needed self-care. The reason I like to treat a cleanse as a retreat is so you can leave behind all the stressors of your routine, such as consuming a processed breakfast sandwich from a café; eating while standing up and holding your child; working long hours and not sleeping; drinking or otherwise indulging too much; or fighting with your partner. All of us have unhealthy patterns and cycles, and a cleanse—especially a cleanse retreat—helps us drop everything to reset our minds, which in turn upsets our routines and interrupts bad habits. Giving yourself the time to reflect and see your world more objectively is a powerful motivator for change, and we don't often afford ourselves a view from that vantage point. When we do cleanse retreats, we're not "in it."

Instead, we are removed from the daily grind and looking at our lives through a calmer, more compassionate lens. We can figure out how to make better decisions for happier lives.

To appreciate how my cleanses work, it's helpful to understand how TCM views health as a holistic system. Many Westerners think that a cleanse is either just a feel-good, pampering ritual or a painful process during which you suffer through drinking dirt-like concoctions. Sure, it can be both of those things in particular circumstances. But in my experience, deep healing can be realized from an exercise like this. Students of Chinese medicine learn that our emotions affect us in specific physical ways; so specific, in fact, that we can pinpoint particular organs or ailments according to our most prevalent emotions. For example, feelings of sadness and grief are related to the lungs, while irritability and anger are connected to the liver. We look at the body as a whole system that works together, so balance is key. Disease can manifest from an unhealthy diet, repressed emotions, a weak immune system, and lack of exercise (also known as qi stagnation, which I'll discuss in a moment). In TCM, all kinds of lifestyle factors play into the greater mixture and affect overall balance.

How does TCM diagnose ailments?

Many factors help practitioners of Chinese medicine diagnose where imbalances lie, but the indicators are different from what is used in the West. For example, the methods a TCM practitioner uses to diagnose your constitution or investigate an ailment might range from taking your pulse and looking at the texture, shape, and color of your tongue, to studying your face and eyes. Although these methods might seem odd to Westerners, they are reliable ways a TCM practitioner can detect signs of imbalance, which is the key indicator of disease, pain, or sickness in the body. The most common way to think about it is to imagine a state of stagnation, where the traffic systems of the body are at a standstill, rather than flowing freely. As an example, if you have too much heat in your body because of an infection, you will most likely have a red face and tongue, a rapid pulse, and complain of a fever. By treating the heat with cooling foods, acupuncture points, and herbs, the heat, which is the infection, will be effectively cleared.

Qi, the life force

The Eastern system of medicine is based on the idea of *qi* (pronounced "chee"), which means energy. In the Chinese concept of the universe,

qi is everywhere, flowing around and through us. Feng shui—the Chinese practice of configuring a physical space, such as a home or office, to direct positive energy around it—is also based on the principles of qi. When it comes to our bodies, we can employ such Eastern practices as yoga and martial arts to stimulate qi flow for better physical and mental balance.

When there's imbalance in the body, an Eastern practitioner will determine the root cause of the imbalance and figure out where and why the qi is stuck. Is it in the liver? Is there a deficiency in the spleen? Through the study of TCM, I have learned how to determine the presence of an imbalance and remove stagnation through all manner of holistic healing tools. Any number of signs can point to imbalance, and each is related to a particular organ system. It's a very different medical approach from what Westerners are used to, but once you begin to

HOT VS. COLD BODY TYPES IN TCM

Yang / Hot Body Type	Yin / Cold Body Type
PERSONALITY TYPE	
○ Tends to be outgoing	○ Tends to be introverted
○ Tendency for an aggressive personality	○ Has a quiet personality
○ Easy to anger or irritate	○ Slow to anger
PHYSICAL SYMPTOMS	
○ Red complexion	○ Pale complexion
○ Usually feels hot	○ Usually feels cool or cold
○ Desires cold liquids	○ Prefers warm liquids
○ Strong appetite	○ Weak appetite
○ Prone to constipation and dark urine	○ Prone to loose stools, copious urination
○ Tends to have a loud voice	○ Tends to have a weak voice
FOODS THAT HELP	
○ Fresh fruits	○ Ginger, garlic, green onions
○ Juices	○ Black beans
○ Green and other vegetables	○ Sesame seeds
FOODS TO AVOID	
○ Hot, spicy foods	○ Cold, raw foods

learn this system, you will discover that you can help heal yourself using natural ingredients to treat your condition. Signs of imbalance can appear as the result of any number of situations, from poor diet and extreme stress to a hectic lifestyle, emotional turmoil, and, maybe most importantly, repressed emotion. The latter is one of the most common root causes of illness I encounter, and it usually shows up with some apparent imbalance in your typical constitution, that is, your body's standard way of being.

The body's constitution

In Chinese medicine, your constitution refers to your physical makeup and tendency. It reveals the complete picture of your health on any given day: what sorts of ailments you're prone to, your typical body temperature, your natural immunity, and your emotional state. With a few diagnostic tools borrowed from the TCM tradition, you can begin to assess what category you fit in, and then use diet and lifestyle recommendations to stay in balance. Of course, Chinese medicine is a complex system and everyone has a unique state with complex particular factors. Please know that what I'm sharing is only a very high-level guideline. If you're interested in learning more about TCM and want a thorough diagnosis, visit a certified TCM practitioner who can employ a wide range of diagnostic tools to arrive at a correct evaluation. For our purposes here, you can determine which factors are familiar to you, and which foods treat common ailments. By using the Glossary of Healthful Properties of Common Foods (SEE PAGE 106) and the list of Specific Ailments and Foods That Treat Them (SEE PAGE 117), you'll have the tools you need

to start choosing specific foods to help heal myriad conditions.

For thousands of years, people knowledgeable about TCM have used foods to help harmonize the body. The energetic properties of foods can be potent medicine, and nutrition is the one of the primary ways that the Chinese population practices preventative health care, heals ailments, and stays balanced. Chinese nutrition looks at the energetic properties of foods for their qualities, such as cooling, drying, or warming. For example, someone who has terrible PMS and the associated symptoms may have liver qi stagnation. With acupuncture, diet, and herbal therapy we can move the stuck liver energy, thus reducing or eliminating the difficult monthly signs and symptoms of PMS. When you think about ailments that way, the Chinese approach makes sound sense.

Western medicine starts with a symptom and treats that symptom. You have a bruise, so you'll apply something topical or just wait for it to heal. In TCM, a bruise is seen not just as a pooling of blood from trauma, but also as a place of stagnation. The blood is literally stagnating there. By stimulating the qi energy, either through nutrition, blood-moving herbs, or a physical practice like acupuncture, you are able to move the energy, to move the blood, and to reestablish balance and flow, thus clearing up the bruise. Chinese medicine looks at the whole being and where the imbalance originates, in order to create a level of homeostasis and optimal health and well-being. The root cause of the symptom often starts with your constitution and your overall balance, which takes into account physical, mental, and

continued on page 32

THE FIVE TASTES

In addition to eating foods that suit your constitution, it's important to balance your diet with foods from all tastes. The Chinese system holds that there are five flavors of foods, and eating too much of any one flavor can create an imbalance. Unless you are working with a Chinese medicine practitioner and acupuncturist, just keep it simple. For example, say you had a little too much to drink last night. Go for some sour and bitter foods the next day. Feeling tired and sluggish? Don't overdo the sweets and add some bitter foods to your diet. Play around and see what flavors react the best with your body. Again, if you'd like to learn more about this approach, a licensed TCM practitioner can create a customized plan to suit your particular constitution. Here's an overview of the five flavors and their principle properties from a health perspective.

SOUR FOODS /

Sour foods act as an astringent and have a calming, cooling effect on the liver. They are good for diarrhea, profuse sweating, and hemorrhoids. They're also beneficial for those who eat a high-fat, rich diet. Examples include lemon, lime, vinegar, tomato, orange, pickles, and kiwifruit.

BITTER FOODS /

This group of foods dries dampness (think conditions like edema, candida, and cystic acne) and clears heat, especially in the heart. These foods are good for water retention, canker sores, nightmares, heart palpitations, anxiety, and insomnia. Examples include pomelo, burdock root, romaine lettuce, dandelion greens, and other bitter green vegetables.

SWEET FOODS /

Foods that are considered sweet help to tonify the body and, in small amounts, can increase a weak constitution. They also calm the body. People who will benefit the most from sweet foods are thin, have poor digestion due to an imbalance in the spleen and stomach, and have dry skin, hair, and eyes. Examples include sweet foods containing any sweetener (sugar, maple syrup, honey, and the like), sweet fruits, sweet potatoes, rice, almonds, and walnuts.

PUNGENT FOODS /

This food class gets the circulation going and warms the body. Good for a cold, flu, or lung infection, pungent foods make you sweat. Pungent foods are great for stuck energy in the body, evidenced by conditions like bruises, cramping, back, neck, or joint pain, cold, or flu. They are also perfect cold-weather foods and are recommended for people who are overweight or feel tired and sluggish. Examples include mint, garlic, ginger, and pepper.

SALTY FOODS /

Salty foods soften and disperse masses like tumors, nodules, cysts, and cataracts. They also promote healthy bowel movements. Examples of salty foods are seaweed, gluten-free tamari, miso, and all table salts. I recommend avoiding regular iodized table salt and choosing sea salt, Himalayan pink salt, Hawaiian black or pink salt, French gray salt, or any other unprocessed salt; that is, any salt that has not been stripped of its natural minerals.

continued from page 28

emotional states. To expound on that further, a bruise may originate from an imbalance in the liver, digestive system, or spleen. In contrast, a headache could easily be the result of emotional upset, so TCM starts there—at the root of the problem. Although we Westerners would pop a pain pill to ease the headache, Eastern practitioners will determine what caused the headache and use acupuncture, herbal medicine, diet therapy, massage, and/or cupping and moxibustion to treat it.

What is my constitution?

Everything is based on the idea of balance, and if you've ever looked at Eastern art or physical practices, you've surely seen the ubiquitous symbols of yin and yang. From the Eastern perspective, everything in the universe is determined by these two opposing principles, which are feminine and masculine in nature and represent the dark and light, cold and hot, inward and outward, respectively—all the binary dualistic forces that rule our world. So, in the simplest approach to TCM, we'd start by assessing your yin and yang energies. The ideal state, of course, is to be in perfect balance, but many of us lean more in one direction than the other.

Emotions rule the body

More often than not, when I meet and treat people with chronic disease, they relate some part of their illness to repressed pain, anger, or unresolved issues. Even if they don't study TCM and understand the medical tradition that would support their theories, they seem to know intuitively that their repressed emotion has

contributed to their imbalance. I can't tell you how prevalent this is and how much I believe to my core that our emotional condition is a huge factor at the root of our health. In order to truly be healthy, we have to face our emotions, process and release our pain, confront our longstanding issues, and find peace with others and ourselves. It's not easy. It's painful. Sometimes it is a lifelong process, but it's one we can always strive to improve.

It would be easy to preach that emotions are at the root of our health and ask you to accept it blindly, but I know that it is an off-putting concept to some readers. Many people are skeptical of what they perceive to be New Age, and I get that. But my tradition is informed by centuries-old medical practice, not some unfounded invention. So I'd like to share a personal story that illustrates the reason I am convinced of the mind-body-spirit connection. On one hand, I believe it wholeheartedly because my studies made sense to me logically, and my training provided countless examples of the efficacy of TCM. Yet it was a personal experience that showed me not only the mind-body-spirit connection, but also that we are connected to others around us. I know that my emotions contribute to my physical health, and that unseen energies play a very real part in my state of being.

MY STORY In 2006, I was living the good life in San Francisco, where I had a thriving acupuncture practice. I was doing what I loved, I was surrounded by people l adored, and all was good. I was meditating every day, I had a job I was passionate about where I got to help people, and I had a great social life.

In May of that year, one of my best friends, Simmone, who lived in Germany and was visiting for a couple of months, was staying with me. We were having a blast going to amazing dinners, working hard, and laughing a lot. It was a time of pure joy. On this particular morning, I woke up late and was rushing to make it to my office to see my first patient. I jumped into the shower at 8:15 knowing I had to be at work at 8:45, so it would just be a quick rinse. I was washing my face, and when I looked down at my hands I saw that they were covered in blood. My heart was racing and I didn't know where the blood was coming from. I called Simmone in and she couldn't tell either. It seemed like it must be my mouth and nose, but there was no injury or pain. I jumped out of the shower feeling panicked, and the bleeding stopped just as quickly as it had started. I got dressed and rushed to work.

I had seen patients all morning and was experiencing a strange and uncharacteristic irritability. I remember feeling annoyed in my treatment room, which was not the norm for me. Finally, it was lunchtime, and I was in the break room when my phone rang. It was my dad's girlfriend and, as I had missed a call from him the night before, I thought it might be important. I answered the phone and heard crying on the other end. At that moment I knew something really bad had happened. I felt it in my bones. I asked what was wrong, what had happened. She could hardly talk. I asked if my father was okay and she said, "No, honey. Something really bad happened. There was an accident." At that moment it felt like I got punched in the stomach. Instinctively, I ran out of the building. The pain I felt was unbearable and I could hardly move.

"What do you mean?" I yelled. She said, "Your dad is not okay. He died in a car accident." Most everything after hearing those words became a blur. I called my mom to tell her, and I was so upset, she couldn't understand me. I threw the phone on the ground and collapsed. My whole world just stopped in an instant. Thankfully, Simmone and my mom arrived within thirty minutes to get me out of there and care for me.

My relationship with my father was very special; he was my best friend. We had traveled the world together, and he was my true confidant. I could talk to him about anything. He taught me many important life lessons about never judging others, about living and thinking outside of the box. He was a real renaissance man, a true artist.

Later that day, I went to my father's home looking for something of his and a woman friend of his said to me, "Neka, don't look for anything. Your father has a message for you, and he doesn't want you to worry about anything." At that very moment, I reached down into a box of books, picked one up, and opened to a random page. There, in his handwriting in the margin, it said, "Neka The love of my life. Miss her so. Love her Love her." I was stunned and shaken! That book was fifteen years old, and my father had kept it on his sailboat, writing that note many years earlier. I couldn't believe that at the exact moment someone told me my father had a message for me, I opened a book and actually read his note to me from years earlier. To this day, that confluence of events still blows my mind.

Later that night, the highway patrol called me to ask some questions and give me the details about his accident. They said there was a witness and it had happened at exactly

8:15 a.m. My father had died instantly due to major trauma. I flashed on being in the shower at 8:15 that morning and the unexplained blood. Then I began to shake. At that moment, I knew it was because we were so incredibly connected. My body reacted in a physical way to the major energetic shift that happened when he was taken.

For the next year, my life was all about pain—deep emotional pain and sadness. I remember walking in my neighborhood and seeing people laughing and thinking to myself, they have no idea the depths of anguish life can bring. Every time my phone rang, my heart would begin to pound, thinking someone was calling with bad news. It took months for me to feel even halfway normal. The beautiful part of this experience was all the love and support I received from friends, family, and coworkers. People took care of me through my grief process, holding me when I thought the tears would never end. Now, years later, I know the depth of pain this situation created in my life made me a much deeper and more compassionate person. I know true pain and heartbreak and I know that those who are suffering need love and acceptance. There is so much more to this story, from death and suffering to healing and the birth of my son Frankie, my father's namesake. But that's another book for another day.

I can't explain what happened around my father's death, and I don't feel that I need to. I am not suggesting anything supernatural, particularly as it relates to a cleanse. But I am saying, for me, energy seems present in potent ways that can affect us physically, or in ways we don't understand. I don't know what led that friend of my father's, whom I'd never met before, to say that my father had a message for me.

I don't know why at that exact moment, I opened that book to that page. I don't know why I got a nosebleed at 8:15 a.m., the exact time my father died. I am only saying that I believe that the interconnectedness of all things—and the subtle energies that swirl around us—is personal. The last time I saw my father, he had stopped by my workplace and we had a quick lunch. We had a wonderful conversation. The waitress, who was also a patient of mine, commented on how wonderful it was to see a father and daughter who were seemingly so close and having so much fun together. My father said, "Look at my daughter. I'm so proud of the person she is and I'm so lucky to have her in my life." I can't help but think how serendipitous it was that the last conversation we shared expressed something so meaningful. My understanding of energy is partially academic, from my studies of TCM, but it's also the most real thing I've ever known. We experience serendipity and we feel it. We are guided by intuition. Being aware of—and attuned to—the connections around you is not only important for your health but also for living an examined, rich life.

Because energy connects us all, it is important to be loving in your community. Your negative emotions affect your friends and family. There are millions of stories like mine. Maybe you've thought of someone and then he or she called, or you've run into a friend halfway across the world. We often chalk it up to coincidence, but I believe there are unseen energetic connections among us, and maybe sometimes when we tug that thread by focusing our energy and intention or love toward someone or something, there is an unconscious response. I can't see it or prove it, but I have noticed that, when I'm more centered and living in a compassionate and loving way, life feels like it flows more smoothly. When I engage in behaviors or relationships that aren't healthy, I see more blockages come up in my life. For centuries, Chinese medicine has been based around these very unseen energies.

The good news is, you don't have to adopt my life outlook. I'm just sharing my approach and giving some context for what I mean by energy. Whatever your belief system, you will benefit from setting aside some personal time. It's so easy to walk through our days with blinders on, going through the motions, cruising on autopilot. But I'm here to help you wake up, take stock, dive deep, and reset your mind, body, and spirit so you can have the happiest, most satisfying life possible, and the best relationships with people and events around you. Claim your life and demand the best for yourself.

Doing a cleanse is your first step toward evaluating your health and taking the time to look inward and honestly assess how you are handling all you contain. Walt Whitman said, "I contain multitudes"—a wonderful sentiment about the complexity in each one of us. But that complexity cuts both ways: it is rich and it is heavy. We must celebrate our experiences and ourselves, and we must also examine what it is we hold onto that may be doing us harm. It takes bravery to confront our demons and reflect on past trauma, but it's the only way to let go of the negative feelings and energy that stagnate and cause tension or ultimately disease.

I'd like to share another real person's story with regard to whether negative energy can bring on disease. I had a patient who developed breast cancer. After a long battle, she went into remission and that year she invited me to her birthday gathering at the beach with all her friends. I wasn't going to go, but then, at the last minute, I decided to attend. On my arrival, I overheard my name. Standing with friends around the bonfire, she said "I want to thank Neka because her healing techniques treated my cancer." I was shocked. We had never discussed her perspective in that way, and here she was expressing this powerful emotion and attributing her healing to me.

RENÉE When Renée was diagnosed with breast cancer in 2006, she went into a state of shock. There had been no cancer in her family, she had been raised in a household where health food was regularly served, and she had eaten a vegetarian diet most of her childhood. She was also extremely athletic and had been healthy all of her life. Renée was sure the diagnosis was a mistake. But it was not a mistake. She had breast cancer, so she came to see me. I was Renée's acupuncturist, healer, and friend. I helped her get centered and grounded during a time of great panic and despair. During her first acupuncture treatment, I asked her to identify the things that could help her heal. At that moment, it became clear to her that her tight circle of friends—their love and support—would be a key to her survival. I also encouraged Renée to trust her instincts. She ended up deciding against many Western medicine treatment recommendations, but she did it with the confidence that her choices were right for her body. She saw me twice weekly for acupuncture; switched to a low-sugar, no-alcohol diet; began exercising regularly; and tried to reduce stress in her life as much as possible. Renée felt amazing during this time, but it was a lifestyle that was, for her, hard to maintain because, honestly, "it was not much fun." Since then, she has learned to relax more and not to deprive herself of too many of the things that she loves. She has come to understand that balance is the key to a better lifestyle. Renée also knows that she must take charge of the things that she can control, and that DNA, which plays a huge role in health, is something beyond her control. Renée is no different from the rest of us. We all hang onto painful memories, regrets, sadness, and anger. And when we are out of balance, it can manifest in a number of physical and emotional states. If Renée believes her cancer was partially due to repressed pain, who am I to say otherwise? Our intuition is a powerful thing. Mind you, I'm not saying that emotions equal cancer. I'm saying if you're predisposed to cancer, negative emotions coupled with an unhealthy diet may play a role in triggering the disease. I believe our negative emotions put us in a state of imbalance, which is a state where disease can flourish.

So now that we've talked about the idea of imbalance as a precursor to disease, let's look at common signs of imbalance in the body. If you experience any of these conditions on a regular basis, you will absolutely benefit from a cleanse.

Common Signs of Imbalance

- Irritability
- Frustration
- Sighing
- Tendency to hold emotions in, worrying about other people's feelings more than your own
- For women: PMS, more clotting in menstrual flow, irregular or painful menstruation, sore breasts, migraines, poor digestion, bloating
- Anxiety
- Heavy head
- Cannot think straight
- Feeling like body is holding excess weight
- Poor digestion
- Foggy thinking
- Loose stools
- Indecisive, confused
- Feeling hot in the afternoon and flushed
- Dry skin, dry eyes, dry hair
- Night sweats, hot flashes
- Not feeling 100 percent vibrant, energetic

The amazing thing is, many of us go through life feeling lots of these things, lots of the time. We come to accept that being anxious, irritable, bloated, and exhausted is a way of life. But I'm here to tell you, it doesn't have to be that way. Our bodies are amazing, resilient engines, and when we keep them in balance—with proper nutrition, sleep, and good emotional health—we wake up with energy, stay motivated, and feel hopeful and happy. That's actually our natural state when our bodies are in balance. So many of us have forgotten what that feels like that we see simple joy and lightheartedness as a long-forgotten way of being, as something unattainable in our current state. But a cleanse can help you reset that meter and regain some of your natural lightness. After all, life is short, so why not live the best life you can?

Of course, it's normal to have down times. Light wouldn't exist without dark. You need sadness to have joy. That's the yin and yang of everything. But my study of Eastern medicine has taught me that we should gauge good health and balance by above-average good feeling much of the time.

Time to take responsibility

It's easy for us to get into a routine of blaming our ill health on other people or outside factors. I've been there. It's my oppressive boss, my small-minded boyfriend, my awful upbringing. And to a point, these things do affect us. But in the end, your life is no one's responsibility but yours. Your life is your responsibility. If your job is hellish, maybe you need to consider finding a different one, which may require taking a pay cut, moving, or downsizing your home. Those are big changes that require a brave outlook and a hopeful attitude. But when your happiness and health are at stake, those changes may be worth it. If your relationship is miserable, you may need to walk away from it and face the scary unknown of being single for a while. Or maybe you'll decide to seek counseling together. Only you can set the wheel in motion for whatever it is that can make your bad situation better.

Many of us stay mired in toxic situations because the thought of rocking the boat is overwhelming. And when we get stuck in bad patterns, we grow resentful, projecting our unhappiness outward, making regrettable decisions, and creating a cycle of misery. It's healthy to feel your feelings, but it's not healthy to drown in them and see yourself as an eternal victim. Take control of your life. If you are engaging in behaviors that are putting negative energy out, it will continue to surround you and come back at you. People feel it and avoid it, or push it back toward you.

Doing a cleanse is the perfect opportunity to take stock and ask yourself the hard questions. Be honest and assess where you can improve things for yourself, even if it takes some courage. Love yourself and know your worth. Ask where you've failed and forgive yourself, with a promise to move forward in a better way. Demand better for yourself and do what it takes to make it happen. That's when your life will change.

You can do this!

Wanting to feel better is the first step to making it happen. My goal is to make you feel amazing physically, mentally, and emotionally. I want to help you get out of your rut, assess life's hurdles, and basically prepare you for the Olympics of overwhelmedness. Doing this cleanse is step one in what may be a ten-step process. It may take a year or more to get where you need to be. But doing a cleanse is your chance to pinpoint the condition, identify the feelings, write the journals, set the goals, and ask the questions that will take you where you need to be. You are literally taking the time to look at your life, assess it, and create a game plan to improve it, all the while fortifying your body to strengthen both your health and your resolve. This may mean finding the mental clarity to figure out how to get some counseling, how to move or change jobs, or how to make a change in your relationship. These are hard tasks we deny and put off and avoid—sometimes until we get sick. I'm inviting you to seize the day and demand the best for yourself right now. And I'm going show you how, step by step.

PREPARING FOR YOUR CLEANSE

The first thing I want to put out there, before we get into shopping lists and recipes, is this: be mindful at every stage of the process. This starts with the ingredients you choose. Doing a cleanse isn't just about chucking healthy foods into a blender. It's about careful planning, taking the time and energy to research and choose the best ingredients you possibly can. That's part of the process. I'm going to ask you to choose organic ingredients whenever possible, even if you don't do so in your everyday life. Some people think organic is just code for expensive. It's not. So before we get into the nitty-gritty of your preparations, let me share some basic points that explain my philosophy on organic foods.

Why Organic?

There is an active debate these days about whether or not organic foods are superior to conventionally grown foods. While I do keep up on the current research on the subject, I am already firm in my belief that organic fruits and vegetables are the best choice for your overall health. Here are five reasons why I believe this to be true.

1. It is better for you. Organic food is just as nature intended it. That means it's untainted by chemicals or growth hormones and is neither artificially ripened nor genetically engineered. If the point of the cleanse is to rid the body of toxic substances, it defeats the purpose to consume produce that has been sprayed with chemicals.

2. In some cases, it's nutritionally superior. While studies differ on whether organic produce is generally nutritionally superior, research does show certain instances where particular nutrients are higher. For example, a team of ecologists, soil scientists, horticulturists, farming experts, bioscientists, statisticians, food scientists, pharmaceutical scientists and environmental geneticists found that vitamin C was higher in organic strawberries, possibly an effect of healthier soil with micronutrients superior to fertilizers and chemical soils. According to the Organic Trade Association, "growing crops in healthy soils results in food products that offer healthy nutrients. There is mounting evidence that organically grown fruits, vegetables, and grains may offer more of some nutrients, including vitamin C, iron, magnesium, and phosphorus, and less exposure to nitrates and pesticide residues than their counterparts grown using synthetic pesticides and fertilizers."

The truth is, we need more studies in this area, but I'm a firm believer that nature's system is perfectly designed for what we need. I just don't believe that something made in a lab is superior to what comes out of the ground. Plus, organic food won't be genetically modified with GMOs that have been linked to cancer.

Additionally, organic food in your market is more likely local. So when you're buying food that's shipped in from somewhere else, you're looking at 2 to 3 days travel time, in which food can lose nutritional value. Just another reason I try to buy local, organic whenever possible. And if it comes from a farmer's market, all the better. Sometimes I can find produce picked that same day—still bursting with vitality.

Urban Remedy methods and ingredients are certified by California Certified Organic Farmers (CCOF), the leading organization for promoting and educating about organic farming. To learn more, visit *ccof.org*.

3. It is safer for people. A number of studies have been conducted about whether or not organic fruits and vegetables are better for you than conventionally grown produce. The results are mixed, but I truly believe that organic food is better for you. My personal choice is to avoid pesticides altogether, especially considering that some other recent studies have shown the damage that pesticides can cause, including DNA damage, depression, and Parkinson's disease. Above all, I just feel better knowing that my food, the food I feed my family, and the food I recommend to my clients is as pure as nature intended.

4. It is safer for the planet. When it comes to farming, organic methods protect the environment by building up organic matter in the soil and mimicking natural systems rather than relying on synthetic fertilizers and pesticides. They use less energy and oil. They also protect water resources by refusing chemicals that can contaminate the water supply. Compared with soils on conventional farms, organically farmed soils have been shown to have less nitrogen leeching, better nutrient-holding ability, more efficient biological nutrient cycling, and less runoff and erosion.

5. And, quite simply, it tastes better. When you eat food straight from the ground that has not been grown from genetically modified seeds or treated with synthetic pesticides or fertilizers, artificial additives, or chemical preservatives, guess what? It tastes good. Sweet, strong flavors come through in their natural perfection. Try an organic tomato off the vine and then bite into a mealy supermarket fruit that has been supersized by science. There is simply no comparison.

So for every reason, from health to the environment to great taste, plan to eat organic while on the cleanse, if not all the time. I know that organic foods cost more, so if you can't adopt them all the time, I understand. But for these four days, do your best to buy untainted produce. I promise, it makes a big difference. Remember, too, even though it is organic, you must rinse produce well before using.

Supplies

Before you begin your cleanse, it's a good idea to gather all of the supplies you need in advance so that, during the 4-day period, all you need to focus on is detoxifying your mind and body. I've divided the supplies into two lists: equipment and ingredients. The equipment list outlines both tools you'll need to prep food as well as items useful for the cleanse activities. The ingredients list includes edible items as well as items you'll need for your daily healing baths (which you can find at a health food store). I haven't included standard kitchen items, such as measuring cups, mixing bowls, and wooden spoons, as I assume most households are already equipped with them. That said, you may want to scan the lists for for the cleanse days (PAGES 56-99) and to make sure your kitchen has the needed staples.

The first two items on the equipment list are a blender and a juicer, and despite what some people believe, they are not interchangeable. You cannot make juice in a blender, and you cannot make smoothies in a juicer. So while these items may seem redundant, they are, in fact, very different machines for different purposes. And you will need both for this cleanse. The good news is that you probably already have a blender and many of the other tools you'll need, like a salad spinner and a garlic press. In other words, although the equipment list looks long, you probably won't have to buy much. Finally, the juicer is your main investment for the program, and you'll be buying a relatively small amount of food, so consider whatever you pay out of pocket to be a replacement for the bread, meat, beer, and sweets you would otherwise be purchasing over those days.

Equipment

Here is a list of the kitchen, bath, and other equipment you'll need for your four-day cleanse.

BLENDER / A blender is for blending whole ingredients, and is necessary for smoothies, sauces, and other puréed mixtures. I like a high-speed blender like those made by Vitamix and Blendtec. But these are admittedly professional-grade machines, and you can make my recipes with whatever blender you have at home. If you want a less expensive option, look for a mini blender. I do advocate investing in a better-quality model, so that it will last for a while, but you must do what your budget allows. I prefer a high-speed blender for both consistency and texture. It also helps with flavor. For example, if you're using cinnamon and vanilla bean, it binds flavors and breaks up chunks better. So, if your pocketbook can handle the cost, opt for a high-speed machine.

JUICER / A juicer extracts juice from fruits and vegetables like apples, beets, carrots, and kale. The more powerful your juicer, the more nutrients and value you'll get from each item. There are two kinds of juicers to choose from, and either one will work for the cleanse.

Cold-press juicers are designed to slowly and gently squeeze the maximum amount of nutrients out of each ingredient. That makes them ideal for cleansing or making nut milks and green juices. They cost more than centrifugal juicers, but because they work slowly and efficiently to extract the most nutrients and do not heat the juice, they preserve vitamins, enzymes, and trace minerals. Cold-pressed juices can be sealed in airtight bottles and

refrigerated for up to seventy-two hours without losing any nutrient content. In this category, Hurom makes a reliable model for home use.

Centrifugal juicers use a spinning metal blade and a mesh filter to pulverize the produce and pull juice outward by means of centrifugal force. They are less expensive than cold-press juices and extract less juice. Their action creates a small amount of heat, which can destroy some of the rich enzymes and thus impact the overall nutrient content of the juice. That said, you're still getting 100 percent fruit and vegetable matter and that can only do you good. Centrifugal juicers create a fair amount of foam, and the juices oxidize more quickly, so you'll want to drink them immediately, before they lose more precious nutrient content through aeration. In this category, I like Breville juicers for home use.

In my work, I use a professional-grade juicer for maximum nutrient extraction, but I understand that individuals are on a budget. I recommend spending no less that $100, though you can find a juicer for half that price.

SALAD SPINNER / A salad spinner is not mandatory, but it sure does make washing salad greens easier. That's important because it is a task we're going to do mindfully and carefully to make sure we rid the greens of any soil or sand. Wet lettuce dilutes the salad dressing, which ruins the salad. If you prefer to wash and dry your greens by hand, by all means, do so.

GARLIC PRESS / Like the salad spinner, a garlic press is and optional piece of equipment for the cleanse. If you don't mind chopping your garlic cloves into very, very tiny pieces, you can skip it. But this handy, easy-to-use kitchen tool will save you a good deal of prep time and is very affordable.

NUT-MILK BAG / A nut-milk bag helps filter nut meal from the liquid when you make your own nut milk. Look for a reusable one at a health food store or online. In a pinch, you can use an everyday fine-mesh sieve to strain nut milk, but the texture will not be as smooth as that strained through a nut-milk bag.

FOOD PROCESSOR, CHEF'S KNIFE, PARING KNIFE, AND CUTTING BOARD / These common kitchen tools may go without saying, but I'm adding them to your list so you can assess and locate everything you need while you're prepping for your cleanse. A food processor is going to make your life worlds easier for a number of the recipes, so I recommend buying or borrowing one if you don't have one already. You could, in most cases, use a very powerful blender to substitute for this appliance, but you won't achieve the desired effects and textures; try to have a food processor on hand if at all possible.

WATER FILTER / I highly recommend drinking and cooking with filtered water. Again, the point of the cleanse is to give your body a break from chemicals and fluoride and other additives in most drinking water. If you can afford a deluxe filter on your sink, great. But the most economical way to filter water is to use a pitcher filtration system that can be stored in the refrigerator. Or, if you prefer, you can use an ionizer system. I do not advocate buying bottled water, as you'll spend as much on that as on

a pitcher filter system, and the latter is much more friendly to the environment. However you choose to proceed, please use the purest water for drinking and cooking that you can afford.

SOUP POT / A big soup pot is needed to make the medicinal broth that you will be sipping throughout the day. If you don't have a pot that holds at least 5 quarts (5 l) of liquid, consider purchasing one or borrowing one from a friend for your cleanse days.

SPIRAL VEGETABLE SLICER OR SIMPLE MANDOLINE / A spiral vegetable slicer can cut at least three different strips from vegetables: 1/8 inch (3 mm), 1/4 inch (6 mm), and ribbons; it costs slightly more than a basic mandoline, but offers more versatility and appeal. A mandoline is ideal for finely cutting vegetables ultrathin, such as when making zucchini pasta (PAGE 84). You can buy a simple mandoline for under $20.

DRY-SKIN BRUSH / You can find these brushes at most health food or natural food stores. Besides exfoliating and increasing circulation, dry brushing the skin stimulates the lymph system, which is the body's drainage pathway for clearing filtered impurities. It doesn't matter which brand of brush you choose, as long as you make sure it is made with natural, organic materials, especially the bristles.

JOURNAL / You can use any notebook or paper for your journal, but I like the idea of acquiring one especially for this cleanse. This is your retreat, and there's something satisfying about starting a brand-new journal devoted entirely to this project and the goals around it.

Bath ingredients

I recommend a therapeutic bath each night of the cleanse. Here are the ingredients you'll need.

- Fine sea salt or Himalayan pink salt, 1 box (you need at least 1½ lb (750 g)
- Aluminum-free baking soda, 1 box (1 lb/450 g)
- Epsom salts, 1 small carton or bag
- Apple cider vinegar, 1 bottle (16 fl oz/250 ml)
- Hydrogen peroxide, 3 bottles (16 fl oz/500 ml each)
- Ground ginger, 1 small jar (at least 2 oz/60 g)
- Essential oils (optional): Pick one or more oils to add to your bath, both for aromatherapy and for medicinal properties. The oils can be found at health and natural food stores.

  LAVENDER / relaxing, calming, immunity boosting

  PEPPERMINT / eases headache, congestion, fatigue, indigestion, nausea and other stomach issues

  ROSEMARY / antioxidant, antiseptic, astringent, circulation enhancing, helpful for cellulite

  GRAPEFRUIT / reduces appetite, balances mood, fights depression, detoxifies, reduces water retention, cleanses skin

Meal ingredients

This list will allow you to shop just once for supplies before the cleanse, helping you focus on the detox process over the four cleanse days. Remember to buy organic whenever possible.

FRESH PRODUCE

- Apples, Granny Smith, 4
- Apples, Gala, 2
- Avocados, 2–3
- Beet, 1
- Carrots, 22–30
- Celery root, 1–2
- Celery, 2–3 bunches, enough to equal 20 ribs
- Cherry tomatoes, 1 pint
- Collard greens, 1 bunch
- Cucumbers, 6
- Dandelion greens, 1 bunch
- Fennel, 1 bulb
- Flat-leaf parsley, 2 bunches
- Flaxseeds, ground, small bag
- Garlic, 1–2 heads
- Ginger, fresh, 1–2 large clusters (enough to equal 6½–8 inches in ½–1 inch increments)
- Grapefruit, 1
- Green onions, 1 bunch
- Jalapeño chile, 1 (optional)
- Kale, about 4 bunches
- Leeks, 2–4
- Lemons, 4 large or 8 small, plus 9 medium
- Limes, 4
- Mâche, 3 cups (3 oz/90 g)
- Oranges, 2
- Potatoes, white, 2–4
- Purple cabbage, 1 head

- Red bell pepper, 1
- Romaine lettuce, 2 large heads
- Shiitake mushrooms, fresh or dried, 6–12
- Spinach, 6½–11½ cups (6½–11½ oz/ 200–360 g)
- Sprouted raw chickpeas, 1 package
- Sunflower sprouts, 2–3 cups (4–6 oz/125–185 g)
- Sweet potatoes, 2–4
- Swiss chard, 1 bunch
- Turmeric, fresh, 3-inch piece
- Watercress, 1 bunch
- Zucchini, 3

FRESH HERBS
- Basil, 2–3 bunches
- Cilantro, 2 bunches
- Mint, 1 bunch

NUTS AND SEEDS
- Almonds, raw, ¾ cup (3 oz/90 g), plus about 1 cup (5½ oz/170 g) to make almond milk
- Chia seeds, 3 tablespoons
- Hemp seeds, shelled, small bag
- Pine nuts, ¼ cup (1¼ oz/40 g)
- Pumpkin seeds, shelled, small bag
- Sesame seeds, raw, about ¾ cup (3 oz/90 g)

OILS AND VINEGARS
- Cold-pressed extra-virgin olive oil, large bottle
- Cold-pressed flax oil, small bottle
- Cold-pressed sesame oil, small bottle
- Raw apple cider vinegar, small bottle
- Unsweetened rice vinegar, small bottle

MISCELLANEOUS
- Frozen raspberries, small bag
- Frozen wild blueberries, small bag
- Kombu seaweed, 1 bag (7½-by-8 inch/ 19-by-20-cm pieces)
- Miso, soy free, small container
- Nori, 1 bag (7-by-8-inch/18-by-20-cm pieces)
- Sun-dried tomatoes (dry pack), two 3-ounce (90 g) bags
- Wakame seaweed, 1 bag (4-by-1-inch/ 10-by-2.5-cm strips)

SEASONINGS AND SWEETENERS
- Coconut palm sugar, small bag
- Ground cinnamon, 1 small jar
- Ground cumin, 1 small jar
- Liquid stevia, small bottle
- Salt, fine sea
- Salt, Himalayan pink
- Vanilla extract, alcohol free

Phases of your Prep

This phase consists of three parts: dietary prep, mental prep, and scheduling prep. All three sections are essential to ensure that you are prepared to complete the cleanse and make good on the promise you've made to yourself to kickstart your health.

Dietary Prep

To prep for your cleanse, you will start to restrict your diet two to four days in advance to ready the detoxification network. That network includes the following bodily systems: respiratory, gastrointestinal, urinary, skin and derma, lymph, and emotional.

RESPIRATORY / lungs, bronchial tubes, throat, sinuses, and nose

GASTROINTESTINAL / liver, gallbladder, colon, and whole GI tract

URINARY / kidneys, bladder, and urethra

SKIN AND DERMA / sweat and sebaceous glands and tears

LYMPH / lymph channels and lymph nodes

EMOTIONAL / expressing emotions, connecting with your feelings

When you detox your body, you're getting rid of harmful toxins by both transforming them and clearing excess mucus and congestion. The toxins come from the external environment, poor diet, drug use, fats, cholesterol, or free radicals and other molecules that irritate or inflame cells and tissues. If you have trouble digesting, abuse your liver, notice bad skin, get sick a lot, or often feel tired, a cleanse will start to clear these blockages and you'll notice how much better you feel and how much better your body functions.

At the same time, our negative thoughts, emotions, and stress can contribute to toxicity. By giving our organs a break from processed foods and toxins of all kinds, we'll transform ourselves on many levels. Get ready to feel lighter, more open, and have more energy!

You already know to buy organic, and you have your list of equipment and ingredients. Now it's time to prep for your four-day respite from inflammatory foods to cleanse the blood, lymph, liver, kidneys, and colon and to lose a little excess weight. You'll also detox heavy metals and toxins as you alkalinize the body's pH. But diving right into a cleanse can be a shock to the system, so you're going to start a few days in advance by weaning yourself from restricted foods to ease your body into the change. Starting two to four days before your cleanse, please eliminate or greatly reduce consumption of the following items:

AVOID

○ Alcohol

○ Caffeine drinks and coffee*

○ Soft drinks

○ Red meat

○ Cured or processed meat (bacon, sausages, and the like)

○ Nonorganic animal flesh

○ White flour products (pasta, bread, cookies, crackers)

○ Foods that contain hydrogenated fats and preservatives

○ Refined sugars and all products containing them

○ Dairy (milk, cheese)

○ Fried foods

○ All genetically modified foods

○ Canned foods

○ Cigarettes

*If you are accustomed to drinking coffee or black tea every morning and experience withdrawal headaches when you quit, try switching to green tea. There will be no coffee during your four-day retreat, and ideally you will give up coffee a few days prior to the start, so your body isn't hit with every other change at the same time you are experiencing caffeine withdrawal. Stopping caffeine can cause headaches and irritability. Don't be alarmed if you feel a little cranky or headachy when

you cut caffeine out of your day. The effects will pass, and they are just a sign that you're letting your body reestablish its course without additives and stimulants. As with refined sugars, once you have passed the early discomfort period, your dependence and craving will be minimized.

INCORPORATE

- All vegetables, especially those with dark, vibrant colors; think lots of dark green, purple, red, and yellow vegetables

- All fruits

- Sea vegetables

- Grains like brown rice, millet, quinoa, amaranth, and corn

- Any beans or other legumes

- Nuts and seeds

- Chicken, fish, eggs

- Unfiltered cold-pressed flax, olive, sesame, sunflower, almond, coconut, hemp, macadamia nut, and grapeseed oils; try not to heat oils, with the exception of grapeseed and coconut, both of which have a high smoke point

- 8 to 12 glasses filtered water daily

- Fermented foods like miso and sauerkraut

- Probiotic drinks like coconut kefir and kombucha

Mental Prep

Now is also the time to think about setting your intention for the cleanse. Figure out what you hope to get out of this experience and then write it down. Make a list of what you think might be holding you back. It may be obvious or it may involve some painful "getting real" with your current situation and behaviors. Be honest about what you can improve, what you can remove, and where you plan to go. Start to prepare yourself to let go of what's not serving you in your life. By the time you start your cleanse, I would like you to be able to finish this sentence: I am cleansing in order to _____. It might be that you want to detox, let go, lose weight, reset, clear your head for your job or relationship, be better to your kids, treat your health condition—your goal is whatever makes sense in your present life.

Your mental prep should also include creating an intention to nurture your spirit, which is a way to extend your cleanse to your more subtle nature. Our bodies have cellular memory, which means that traumatic or unpleasant experiences can stay with us, stifling our emotional health. So in addition to helping you stay focused and mindful on your cleanse, creating an intention has a more practical purpose: to help you clear the imprint of toxic memories, emotions, or pain, which will help nurture your spirit. Although this is a foreign concept to many in the West, it is something everyone has experienced. Have you ever developed a headache or stomachache as a result of an uncomfortable conflict? This is the mind-body connection in action.

When painful events or difficult emotions aren't released, we hold onto depression, anger, and sadness, all of which can aggravate chronic disease. By creating an intention to eliminate troubling emotions and following through on it, you will be letting go of specific emotional matter that is holding you back from optimal vitality. Maybe you've been ill, suffered a tragedy, or endured a painful divorce. Deciding to cleanse yourself of toxic emotions brought about by such an event is as important as the physical cleanse. Two strategies for setting an intention are meditating on what you want to release or creating affirmations you'll see and say daily to remind yourself of your goals. I also recommend writing down your intention and then burning it in a fire ceremony on completion of the cleanse, thereby releasing it once and for all from your consciousness. I'll talk more on that later, when you get to the cleanse. Rituals like this are important for healing deeply held emotions that can continue to plague you if left unexamined.

Scheduling Prep

To the best of your ability, clear your calendar for the actual four days of the cleanse. If you can't take days off work, at least try to plan part of the program to fall over a weekend. In my ideal world, you'd take off those two extra days from work, so you have four free days to focus on yourself and your experience. Only you know if that's feasible, but if it works for you, I highly recommend treating your cleanse like an actual getaway retreat. It is important to try to remove as much everyday stress as possible, and going to work is definitely a part of that stressful cycle. Regardless of your scheduling, let people know you're doing a cleanse program. Invite friends to join, if you like. It can be inspiring and fun to do it with friends or a partner.

However you proceed, treat yourself to a break from your routine. Carve out time and pretend you're going to a spa. Also, if you find that you are loving the program, there's no reason not to continue beyond four days. Some people stay on the cleanse for a week or more. Others incorporate many of the recipes and practices into their lifestyle indefinitely. You can scale the cleanse to suit your needs and goals.

Your cleanse days at a glance

Despite what you may think, you will be busy preparing foods, juices, baths, and detox applications. You'll likely spend much more time thinking about these types of activities than you do in your normal day-to-day routine, but that's the point. I'm teaching you how to approach food and practices that nurture you, body and soul, mindfully. When you're done with this cleanse, you'll be armed with myriad ways to address ailments, improve your health, and pamper yourself. On each day of your cleanse, you can expect to enjoy the following activities:

○ Making a gratitude list
○ Drinking warm lemon water as soon as you wake up
○ Dry brushing your skin and showering
○ Making and drinking a green juice
○ Making and eating breakfast
○ Enjoying some mineral broth
○ Engaging in a mindful morning activity
○ Making and eating lunch
○ Engaging in a mindful afternoon activity
○ Making and eating dinner
○ Taking a medicinal spa bath, or, if you don't have a bathtub, a foot bath
○ Writing in a journal
○ Practicing a pre-bed meditation (optional)

I am assuming that you're able to carve out time to devote four days to your cleanse, but I'm not insisting that you take time off work. Because there is a good deal of food preparation involved, you'll find it much easier to administer your cleanse at home. That said, it is possible to make your foods the night before and tote them to work, if necessary.

Your Menus at a Glance

DAY 1 /

Lemon water (PAGE 61)

Apple-Ginger Green Juice (PAGE 63)

BREAKFAST Raw Apple Granola with Almond Crème (PAGE 63)

Alkalizing Mineral Broth (PAGE 64) with miso

Immunity Boost juice (PAGE 67)

LUNCH Mâche Salad with Pumpkin and Hemp Seeds (PAGE 67), Turmeric Ginger Lemonade (PAGE 68)

Alkalizing Mineral Broth (PAGE 64) with miso

DINNER Collard Wraps with Basil-Mint-Lime Sauce (PAGE 68)

Alkalizing Mineral Broth (PAGE 64) with miso

DAY 2 /

Lemon water (PAGE 61)

Good Morning Green Juice (PAGE 74)

BREAKFAST Antioxidant Green Smoothie (PAGE 75)

LUNCH Ensalada Verde (PAGE 75)

Alkalizing Mineral Broth (PAGE 64) with miso

DINNER Asian Kale Salad (PAGE 77)

Alkalizing Mineral Broth (PAGE 64) with miso

DAY 3 /

Lemon water (PAGE 61)

Dandelion Liver Tonic (PAGE 82)

BREAKFAST Big bowl of Alkalizing Mineral Broth (PAGE 64) with miso

LUNCH Raw Avocado-Carrot Soup (PAGE 83)

Vital Citrus Juice (PAGE 83)

Alkalizing Mineral Broth (PAGE 64) with miso

DINNER Zucchini Pasta with Tomato Sauce and Pine Nut–Hemp Pesto (PAGE 84)

Alkalizing Mineral Broth (PAGE 64) with miso

DAY 4 /

Lemon water (PAGE 61)

Good Morning Green Juice (PAGE 74)

BREAKFAST Large bowl of Alkalizing Mineral Broth (PAGE 64) with miso

LUNCH Sunflower Sprout and Carrot Juice (PAGE 90)

Tummy Lover Juice (PAGE 93)

Alkalizing Mineral Broth (PAGE 64) with miso

DINNER Mediterranean Mix Salad (PAGE 93)

Alkalizing Mineral Broth (PAGE 64) with miso

YOUR 4-DAY CLEANSE

By embarking on this cleanse, you are giving yourself the gift of health. Each day you will be doing 12 to 15 related steps that will help you along your journey. Look to pages 46–50 for a detailed ingredient and equipment list outlining all the supplies you need to have on hand for the next four days. One of the first tasks on Day 1 is to prepare a beneficial, mineral-rich broth that will help sustain you throughout the cleansing process. Depending on how much broth you consume, you may need to make another batch before your cleanse is over, so bear that in mind when you are planning. Plan to shop or gather all of your items before you begin the cleanse so that you can devote all your energy to the detox. Another word of advice: if you have any medical issues, be sure to check in with a trusted health practitioner before you begin any cleansing program.

CLEANSE / **DAY 1** /

CLEANSE / DAY 1 /

Welcome. You have arrived. Congratulations on starting your cleanse today. Getting here was a matter of planning and preparation, mental and practical. By now you've prepped your body, purchased your ingredients, and gathered your other supplies. You've thought about your reasons for doing a cleanse and maybe started making lists of changes you plan to make and goals you intend to accomplish. Starting this morning, every single thing we do each day will be working toward those goals. So let's get started.

Make your gratitude list

The first thing you're going to do each morning during the four-day cleanse is write down, on a clean page of your journal, everything for which you're grateful. It can be your children, your dog, a great job, friends that make you laugh—anything that makes you smile and feel happy. Focus on the positive things in your life and remind yourself that even when you are challenged, good things are still around you. Think about what they are and practice feeling appreciative of them. If you find yourself in a negative thought spiral, focus on your gratitude for arriving at this place of self-improvement or your newfound commitment to making things better. It's okay if what you're grateful for is simply your decision to do this cleanse.

If for some reason you're not able to write these things down, you can instead focus on them in a meditation. The main goal here is to feel the gratitude. You should always be able to find something worth smiling about, something for which you feel glad. The reason we do this is not only because it's a wonderful way to start the day—it also sets the tone and establishes a positive outlook for the day ahead. And more importantly, some scientific studies have shown that the power of positive thinking can affect our overall health.

Because it is Day 1, I also want you to write down what it is you hope to accomplish by completing the cleanse, in both the short term and the long term. Write down what you would like to achieve at the end of four days, where you see your ideal self in six months, and where would you like to be a few years from now. Thinking about goals in this way helps you take a phased approach that requires patience. Your goals may be something like the following: short term, detox my body; six months from now, be in a new job; a few years from now, be happy in my career and saving enough money to take a great trip annually.

I also like the idea of setting goals because I firmly believe that before you can achieve anything, you have to consciously recognize that you want it. Making these long-term goals establishes that you want these things, the first step toward making them happen. Many of us feel we don't deserve certain things: a promotion, a better relationship, and a healthy self-image.

But setting a goal for yourself is a powerful means of telling yourself you can have it and you intend to do what it takes to get it. Nothing is out of your reach if you set your mind to it.

Drink warm lemon water

In traditional Chinese medicine, the spleen and the stomach are paired organs that regulate digestion. If they're not working properly, you'll feel sluggish and bloated, so it's important to start the day with a system booster. The spleen likes warmth, which makes drinking warm lemon water a great way to alkalinize the body naturally and to stimulate bile production to flush the liver the first thing in the morning. You'll drink the lemon water every morning of your cleanse to get the body ready and revved up for the day.

LEMON WATER

Consuming this warm citrus drink before you do anything else in the morning is a great practice to incorporate into your daily life.

2 cups (16 fl oz/500 ml) filtered water
Juice of 1 large or 2 small lemons

In a saucepan, bring the water to a boil, or nearly to a boil, then let it cool until just warm. Add the lemon juice, then pour into a heatproof glass or mug. Drink the lemon water while it is still warm.

Dry brush your skin and shower

I love this ritual, which is designed to stimulate the lymph system and circulation. In addition to being a great way to dig into your detox, it feels amazing, like an exfoliation and brisk massage all in one. Skin brushing works in a few ways: it exfoliates dead skin cells and promotes cell renewal, it helps the lymphatic system drain and remove toxins, and it aids digestion and kidney function. Some say it also smooths the appearance of cellulite, which is always an appealing benefit.

Using your skin brush with natural bristles (never synthetic), brush your whole body in long sweeping strokes toward your heart. Start at one foot and sweep up to the knee, then up to the thigh, and then repeat first with the other foot and then on the back of each leg. Again, working on one side and then the other, start at the fingertips, sweep up to the elbow, then up to the shoulder. Starting at the pelvis, sweep up the torso and then sweep up the lower back. Give each section a few minutes of attention and you'll be amazed how invigorated your body feels. The brushing will leave your skin feeling tingly and awake.

Now, follow up by rinsing off in a warm (not hot) shower. If you are brave enough, try a brisk, cool rinse for an extra-invigorating experience.

Make your green juice

All right, it's time to make your first green juice. Green juice helps to alkalinize the body. It's cleansing and energizing, saturating the body with essential phytonutrients.

Phytonutrients, which are simply nutrients that come from plants, are some of the most power-packed substances on the planet. They help repair cells, inhibit cancer-causing substances, and fight degeneration in the body. Green juices are especially rich in chlorophyll, a powerhouse healer that cleanses the blood, boosts oxygen, and improves circulatory, digestive, immune, and detoxification systems. So you can imagine why having at least one green juice a day is a potent practice when

Dry brushing your skin every morning helps stimulate your lymphatic system and remove toxins you're cleansing—or for any time you want to boost your health.

For some people, green juice can taste unpleasant, but you'll find that, as you get accustomed to it, the juice will help reset your body so you don't experience sugar or caffeine cravings. Your body will actually start to crave your green juice because it has felt the benefits. Today, you'll start with an "easy" green juice, meaning it's naturally sweetened with apple and flavored with ginger. You'll want to have this one in your regular repertoire because it's as tasty as it is effective. You're going to use your juicer for this recipe, so start by gathering the necessary equipment and prepping all of the ingredients.

APPLE-GINGER GREEN JUICE

This juice is great when you are craving a little bit of sweetness in your day.

- 4 celery ribs
- 1–2 cups (1–2 oz/30–60 g) spinach leaves
- 2 kale leaves
- 1-inch (2.5-cm) knob fresh ginger
- 1 green apple
- ¼ bunch fresh flat-leaf parsley
- 1 cucumber

Cut the vegetables and the apple as needed into pieces that will fit into the chute of your extraction juicer. Then, following the manufacturer's instructions, juice all of the ingredients in the order given. Pour into a tall glass.

Make your breakfast

It's already been a busy morning, and if you're anything like me, you've worked up an appetite. Today we're going to have one of my favorite breakfasts, made from raw fruits and nuts. You won't believe how great it tastes.

RAW APPLE GRANOLA WITH ALMOND CRÈME

Here is a fantastic example of how raw food, chock-full of enzymes and nutrients, can satisfy you with rich, seemingly decadent flavor. Everything in it is good for you: the apples clear heat, protect lungs, and benefit the liver and gallbladder; the almonds, which are particularly rich in vitamins and minerals, temper coughs and asthma symptoms; and the cinnamon helps maintain proper blood sugar levels. I promise that once you try this combination, packaged cereal will never hold the same allure.

FOR THE ALMOND CRÈME

¼ cup Soaked Almonds (page 168)

2 tablespoons Almond Milk (page 142)

1 tablespoon coconut palm sugar, or ½ teaspoon liquid stevia

Pinch of sea salt

FOR THE GRANOLA

2 Gala apples, quartered and cored

½ cup (2½ oz/75 g) Soaked Almonds (page 168)

2 tablespoons freshly ground flaxseeds

½ teaspoon ground cinnamon

Pinch of sea salt

1 tablespoon alcohol-free vanilla extract

A few drops liquid stevia, to taste

To make the almond crème, in a blender, combine all of the ingredients and blend on high speed until smooth. If not serving immediately, cover and refrigerate until needed.

To make the granola, in a food processor, combine the apples and almonds and pulse until coarsely chopped. Transfer to a bowl.

In a small bowl, combine the flaxseeds, cinnamon, salt, vanilla, and stevia and stir to mix well. Sprinkle the flaxseed mixture evenly over the apple-almond mixture. Top with a dollop of the almond crème. Refrigerate any extra almond crème for up to 2 days.

Make your mineral broth

You are now going to make a big batch of mineral broth that will last for your entire four-day cleanse. (Depending on how much broth you sip, you may need to make another batch partway through your cleanse). It's easy to make, but it does simmer for a long time. If you get it going now, you can enjoy it later, after lunch and again in the evening. The mineral broth keeps the stomach and spleen warm, continuing the work the warm lemon drink did earlier. It's a wonderful restorative tonic that helps balance the body's pH, bringing alkalinity back to a normal state and decreasing excess acidity. I like to stir some miso into the broth. It is rich in probiotic substances and helps build the immune system. For more information on miso, turn to page 113.

We tend to eat an acidic diet, high in sugar, sodium, meat, dairy, and alcohol, and this broth can counteract all that acidity by flooding the body with organic minerals, including organic sodium, potassium, and calcium. Overall, it has a purifying effect on the whole body, especially for people who are weak and tired. Best of all, it's surprisingly satisfying when you need a savory snack. I recommend drinking at least 2–3 cups (16–24 fl oz/500–750 ml) a day, and I'll remind you in the afternoon and evening to drink it at junctures when I think it makes sense.

ALKALIZING MINERAL BROTH

This nourishing broth is an essential part of the cleansing retreat. You're going to make your mineral broth in one large batch and consume it at regular intervals over the course of the 4-day cleanse. Each time you're ready to have some broth, bring it to a boil, then let it cool down a bit before stirring in 1 teaspoon of any type of miso, preferably a soy-free variety. In general, I consume about a mug of the broth as a snack. However, in two instances over the four days, you'll sip a bowlful, when the broth is standing in for a meal. I recommend increasing the miso to 1 tablespoon for the mealtime portions.

1 celery root, peeled and quartered

1 carrot, roughly chopped

1 leek, roughly chopped

4 cloves garlic

½ bunch fresh flat-leaf parsley

Skin of 2 white potatoes

Skin of 2 sweet potatoes

4 pieces wakame seaweed, each about 4 by 1 inches (10 by 2.5 cm)

2 pieces kombu seaweed, each about 7½ by 8 inches (19 by 20 cm)

3 green onions, roughly chopped

6 fresh or dried shiitake mushrooms

2-inch (5-cm) knob fresh ginger

1 teaspoon sea salt

Filtered water

4 kale leaves, roughly chopped

In a large, deep stockpot, combine the celery root, carrot, leek, garlic, parsley, white and sweet potato skins, both seaweeds, onions, mushrooms, ginger, and salt and add filtered water to cover. (You will need about 16 cups/4 qt/ 4 l water.) Bring to a boil over high heat, reduce the heat to a simmer, cover, and simmer for 1½ hours.

Remove from the heat and add the kale. In batches, using a ladle, transfer the mixture to a blender and purée until smooth. Let cool, then transfer to an airtight container and refrigerate for up to 4 days.
Makes about 14 cups (104 fl oz/3¼ l)

Alkalizing Mineral Broth

Getting out into nature is an important
part of your 4-day cleanse

Select a morning activity

At this point, I'd like you to check in with yourself and assess how you're feeling. If you like yoga, this is the perfect time to take a class. If you love being in nature, get outside for a brisk walk or invigorating bike ride. If you're feeling tired, relax and read a book. The point is, I'd like you to make the decision mindfully. And I'd like you to avoid television and social media. Pretty much anything with a screen serves as a portal to distraction, conveniently allowing you to escape reality and do the opposite of what the cleanse is about: reflecting on your life and your choices.

Enjoy a late-morning refreshment

This is a refreshing juice that supports your immune system and your cleansing goals overall. Gram for gram, watercress has more vitamin C than oranges and more calcium than spinach, so consuming it is a powerful way to stay strong and supported while you detox.

IMMUNITY BOOST

It you feel like you might be getting sick, this juice will help fight off the illness.

- ½ beet
- 2 kale leaves
- Handful of watercress sprigs
- 1 lemon, peeled
- 1 Granny Smith apple
- 4 carrots

Cut the vegetables and fruits as needed into pieces that will fit into the chute of your extraction juicer. Then, following the manufacturer's instructions, juice all of the ingredients in the order given. Pour into a tall glass.

Make your lunch

For lunch, you are making a mâche salad with pumpkin seeds, hemp seeds, and cilantro and enjoying it with a nutrient-rich spiced lemonade. Mâche is a tender green found in produce stores and many health food stores. If you do not find it, you can substitute arugula or spinach. You will also make a delicious lemonade that incorporates a potent healing spice, turmeric.

MÂCHE SALAD WITH PUMPKIN AND HEMP SEEDS

Mâche, also known as lamb's lettuce or corn salad, is a tender, delicate green, rich in omega-3 fatty acids. Pumpkin and hemp seeds are packed with protein and essential fatty acids.

- 3 cups (3 oz/90 g) mâche leaves
- 3 tablespoons roughly chopped fresh cilantro
- 2 tablespoons pumpkin seeds
- 1 tablespoon shelled hemp seeds

FOR THE DRESSING
- 2 tablespoons fresh lemon juice
- 2 teaspoons cold-pressed extra-virgin olive oil
- 1 teaspoon cold-pressed flax oil
- ¼ teaspoon sea salt
- ¼ teaspoon ground cumin

To make the salad, in a bowl, combine the mâche, cilantro, pumpkin seeds, and hemp seeds and toss to mix.

To make the dressing, in a small bowl, stir together the lemon juice, olive oil, flax oil, salt, and cumin, mixing well. Drizzle over the salad and toss well.

TURMERIC GINGER LEMONADE

Turmeric has long been used in Chinese and ayurvedic medicine to reduce pain and to support digestion and liver health. To keep this powerful anti-inflammatory lemonade a low-glycemic treat, use stevia to sweeten it.

> 2 lemons, peeled
> 1-inch (2.5-cm) knob fresh turmeric
> 1-inch (2.5-cm) knob fresh ginger
> 1½ cups (12 fl oz/375 ml) filtered water
> Liquid stevia to taste

If necessary, cut the lemon into pieces that will fit into the chute of your extraction juicer. Following the manufacturer's instructions, juice the lemons, turmeric, and ginger in that order. Flush the juicer with the water to extract any additional juice from the turmeric and ginger. Pour the juice into a tall glass and stir in the stevia.

Select an afternoon activity

Take a look at the optional activities on pages 97–99 to see if there is something that appeals you. Personally, I love a deeply relaxing and detoxifying castor oil pack treatment. If this were my cleanse, I would do one of these treatments every day at this time while sipping some mineral broth, but it is up to you.

Enjoy an afternoon snack

Bring to a boil a cup of the Alkalizing Mineral Broth (PAGE 64) that you made earlier and stored in the refrigerator. Let it cool slightly, and stir in 1 teaspoon miso. Sip slowly.

> If any of the recipes on this day don't appeal to you, try any green-based juice on pages 130–137; Chia Pudding Parfait (PAGE 127) instead of the granola; or any salad from pages 149–153 for dinner.

Make your dinner

You've had a big day already, and I'm sure you have an appetite, but I hope what you're finding is that the combination of juice, broth, and food is more than enough to satisfy you while also doing your body a world of good. Tonight we're making one of my favorite meals, a Thai-inspired dish with a savory dipping sauce that you will crave postcleanse.

COLLARD WRAPS WITH BASIL-MINT-LIME SAUCE

This nutrient-packed dish will help satisfy your hunger. The tangy, herb-flecked sauce is so delicious, you'll want to use it for other recipes. It is a favorite from my retreats to use as a dressing for green salads or as a sauce for grilled vegetables. You will only need about half of the sauce for this recipe. The remainder can be stored in an airtight container in the refrigerator for up to 4 days.

> FOR THE SAUCE
> 1 cup (8 fl oz/250 ml) fresh lime juice
> 1 clove garlic
> ½-inch (12-mm) knob fresh ginger, peeled and minced
> ½ bunch fresh cilantro
> ½ bunch fresh mint
> ½ bunch fresh basil
> ½ cup (2½ oz/75 g) raw sesame seeds
> 3 tablespoons white or red miso
> ½ cup (4 fl oz/125 ml) filtered water
> 1 teaspoon Himalayan pink salt
> ½ jalapeño chile (optional)
>
> 2 large collard greens, stems removed
> ½ bunch kale, stems removed, leaves finely shredded
> ½ avocado, peeled and thinly sliced
> 1 red bell pepper, halved, seeded, and cut lengthwise into ¼-inch (6-mm) strips
> ¼ cucumber, peeled, halved, seeded, and cut lengthwise into ¼-inch (6-mm) strips

Turmeric Ginger Lemonade

To make the sauce, add all of the ingredients to a high-speed blender and purée until smooth. Pour about ¾ cup (6 fl oz/180 ml) of the sauce onto a plate.

To make a wrap, lay 1 collard leaf horizontally on a work surface, rib side down. In a bowl, toss together the kale and 2–3 tablespoons of the lime sauce, coating the kale evenly. Spoon half of the kale onto the collard leaf, leaving a 1-inch (2.5-cm) border uncovered on all sides. Next, evenly stack half of the avocado, red pepper, and cucumber on top of the kale. Starting from the side nearest you, bring the edge of the leaf up and over the filling, fold in both ends, and then continue to roll tightly to the opposite edge. Place the roll seam side down on a plate. Repeat with the remaining collard leaf and filling ingredients to make a second wrap and add to the plate.

Reserve the remaining sauce for another use, stored in an airtight container in the refrigerator for up to 4 days.

Prepare your medicinal spa bath

Personally, my favorite part of the cleanse day is right before bed, when I get to take a long, dreamy soak. I call these medicinal baths because each day you'll make a new "recipe" of effective ingredients that help you detox the system. That said, baths are a wonderful way to relax and pamper yourself in a spa-like fashion. I've added recommended aromatherapy oils whose fragrance will transport you and add a sensory dimension to the healing bath preparation. Also, I recommend going all out with candles, dim lights, and relaxing music. All of these elements together help ensure an incredible night's sleep. For your first night's bath, I have chosen a simple mix of salt and baking soda, which is detoxifying and will soothe sore muscles. I've also suggested grapefruit essential oil to contribute to

detoxification and cleanse the skin. If you don't have a bathtub, you can enjoy the same benefits by soaking your feet in the same combination of ingredients, using a wide bucket or large bowl. To create a foot bath, divide the ingredients in half and create the same meditative ambiance of candles, music, and/or dim lights that you would choose for your bath. Situate yourself in a comfortable seated position, and relax.

SALT AND SODA BATH

1 cup (7½ oz/235 g) sea salt or Himalayan pink salt

1 cup (7 oz/220 g) aluminum-free baking soda

6 drops grapefruit essential oil (optional)

To make your bath, fill the tub with the hottest water you can stand and dissolve the sea salt and baking soda in the water, swirling it around to be sure all the granules dissolve. Add your fragrance drops, if using, under running water. Soak in the tub for 20 minutes.

Write in your journal

At the end of your first day, I would like you to take some time, maybe 20 minutes, to write down how you're feeling about the day. It can be a major change to begin a cleanse, not only because of the change in diet but also because of all the time spent concentrating on your actions and taking care of yourself. It can have a profound effect that brings up emotion, as you realize how little time you usually spend on self-care. Jot down your thoughts and include how you're feeling mentally and physically, so that you can track the changes over the course of four days. Also, at a later date when you want to remember the process, you will have a good record that you can reread. Try and reflect more deeply on what you are letting go and write down any insights, memories, or solutions so that you can process and release that around which you have created your intention.

OPTIONAL
Enjoy a before-bed treat
Bring a cup of the Alkalizing Mineral Broth that you made this morning (PAGE 64) to a boil, let cool slightly, and stir in 1 teaspoon miso. Sip slowly.

OPTIONAL
Practice a pre-sleep meditation
Sit or lie in a comfortable position and close your eyes.

Take a few deep breaths into your belly, letting yourself relax more deeply with each exhalation.

Intentionally visualize yourself breathing in images of health, love, and acceptance while picturing your exhalations as a release of toxins, negativity, and old patterns that you want to let go.

Continue with the breathing and visualization process until you are in a state of complete relaxation.

Now, imagine you are standing underneath a beautiful waterfall and that clean, clear, refreshing water is flowing down over your whole body. Beginning at the top of your head, imagine the water washing away all of the old ways of thinking that no longer serve you; let the water wash away any blocked energy and then move down into your neck and shoulders, flushing away any aches and pains in your back and down your spine.

Next, imagine the water flowing through your internal organs, flushing out your lungs, stomach, liver, kidneys, and intestines. Imagine the water continuing down your thighs, knees, calves, and through your feet, letting all the excess water flow out of the bottom of your feet, releasing all the negativity deep into the earth.

You may also choose to visualize a white light. Breathe in the love and healing that the light imbues, and then exhale any negativity from your system.

Continue with the practice until you feel that the water (or light) has completely flushed your mind, body, and spirit, and you feel clean, rejuvenated, and grateful for things you have let go. Cultivate a willingness to fill the empty spaces with health, love, and abundance.

LEFT TO RIGHT

Ensalada Verde, Asian Kale Salad, Alkalizing Mineral Broth, Antioxidant Green Smoothie, Good Morning Green Juice

CLEANSE / **DAY 2** /

CLEANSE / DAY 2 /

You did it! One day down; three to go. I hope you're feeling energized and inspired by your first day, and that you are thinking about adding some aspects of this cleanse to your regular routine. Today, you'll be familiar with a lot of the steps so it's a great day to add one of the optional activities if you haven't already tried. This morning, you'll proceed much as you did yesterday, but you'll be making new recipes and reflecting on new insights.

Make your gratitude list

I know you did this yesterday, but I recommend it every day—even when you're not cleansing. New things will occur to you, and as you become more practiced, you may become grateful for hurdles or challenges that have helped you gain insight or grow as a person. When you make your list today, try and sense the gratitude in your body and project it into the world as if you are silently shouting it in the form of positive feeling.

Drink warm lemon water

Follow the instructions on page 61 to make your lemon water. Sip slowly before you do anything else.

Dry brush your skin and shower

Follow the instructions on page 61 to dry brush your skin. Follow with a warm shower and an optional cool rinse.

Make your green juice

Yesterday, I went easy on you with a sweet green drink for your first day. Today, I want you to try a green drink that supports the system by lowering all sugar content, which will contribute to balanced hormones and a balanced endocrine system and will help cut cravings. Besides the health benefit, I would like you to get used to trying unsweetened green juices, so that you become accustomed to the flavor of the vegetables. You will discover that as you try them more and more often, they become more enjoyable. They taste like good health, and believe me, your body will respond! Who knows, you may even start craving them.

GOOD MORNING GREEN JUICE

This is a perfect green juice. It's low in sugar and amazing for your body. Nix the morning-coffee ritual and try an energy-promoting green juice instead. It is light, crisp, and bursting with nutrients.

    4 celery ribs
    1–2 cups (1–2 oz/30–60 g) spinach leaves
    2–4 kale leaves
    ¼ bunch fresh flat-leaf parsley
    1 cucumber, unpeeled

Cut the vegetables as needed into pieces that will fit into the chute of your extraction juicer. Then, following the manufacturer's instructions, juice all of the ingredients in the order given. Pour into a tall glass.

Make your breakfast

For breakfast today, you're going to have a smoothie that's brimming with antioxidants, cancer-fighting nutrients, phytochemicals, and healthful omega-3s. What's great about it is that it is not only good for you but also tastes great.

ANTIOXIDANT GREEN SMOOTHIE

The hefty dose of berries here is what makes this smoothie particularly delicious and satisfying. Wild blueberries have the highest levels of antioxidants, so choose wild over conventional if available.

  1 cup (8 fl oz/250 ml) Chia Gel (below)
  ½ cup (2½ oz/75 g) frozen blueberries, preferably wild blueberries
  ½ cup (4 oz/125 g) frozen raspberries
  Handful of spinach leaves
  2 kale leaves, coarsely chopped
  5–10 drops liquid stevia, to taste (optional)

In a blender, combine all of the ingredients and blend on high speed for 45 seconds. The mixture should be smooth and thick. Pour into a tall glass.

CHIA GEL

  3 tablespoons chia seeds
  2 cups (16 fl oz/500 ml) filtered water

In a small bowl, combine the chia seeds and water and whisk until well mixed. Then repeat the whisking every 30 seconds for 3 minutes to prevent clumping. Store the chia gel in an airtight container in the refrigerator for 3–4 days. Makes a generous 2 cups (16 fl oz/500 ml).

If any of the recipes on this day don't appeal to you, try any green-based juice on pages 130–137; Blueberry Goji Acai Smoothie (PAGE 145) instead of the green smoothie; or any salad from pages 149–153 for dinner.

Go outside for your morning activity

Whether it's a jog around the neighborhood, a short hike, or a bike ride, today I want you to get outside (weather permitting, of course). We spend so much of our time in the office, in the car, or in front of a computer that we sometimes forget to go outdoors and breathe fresh air even once during the day. Make a point to do this today, even if for only a short time.

Make your lunch

For your lunch, you will be drinking what would otherwise be a very large vegetable salad—a whole head of romaine lettuce and a whole cucumber for starters. Run through a juicer, the fresh ingredients are transformed into a glass of pure nutrients that will flood your body with chlorophyll, vitamins, and minerals. You'll feel great as you drink it up.

ENSALADA VERDE

A salad in a glass, this low-glycemic juice is brimming with health benefits.

  4 celery ribs
  1–2 cups (1–2 oz/30–60 g) spinach
  2 kale leaves
  1 head romaine lettuce
  2 Swiss chard leaves
  ¼ bunch fresh cilantro
  ¼ bunch fresh flat-leaf parsley
  1 cucumber

Cut the vegetables as needed into pieces that will fit into the chute of your extraction juicer. Then, following the manufacturer's instructions, juice all of the ingredients in the order given. Pour into a tall glass.

Try a yoga class today as your afternoon activity

Select an afternoon activity

To enhance your cleanse, choose one of the activities that appear on pages 97–99. If it were me, I would select a yoga class or a detoxifying sauna (SEE PAGE 97). Better yet, I'd do both! If you have access to a gym or yoga studio, this is the perfect time to take advantage of its proximity.

Enjoy an afternoon snack

Bring a cup of the Alkalizing Mineral Broth that you made on Day 1 (PAGE 64) to a boil. Let it cool slightly, and stir in 1 teaspoon miso. Sip slowly.

Make your dinner

Dinner this evening is a delicious Asian-inspired kale salad that delivers lots of healing power. Indeed, it is best described as a big plate of medicine for your system.

ASIAN KALE SALAD

Kale is a superfood, full of phytonutrients, and the cilantro is a natural chelator, which means that it helps rid your body of toxic heavy metals. Garlic is an immunity booster, nori supports the thyroid, and avocado is loaded with heart-healthy omega-3 fats. Amazingly, when you put all of these good-for-you ingredients together, you also have one of the best salads you'll ever eat. The key to this salad is to cut the kale very finely so its rough texture disappears.

½ cup (2 oz/60 g) finely chopped carrots

1 tablespoon black sesame seeds

2 tablespoons rice vinegar

½ cup (1½ oz/45 g) finely chopped purple cabbage

1 tablespoon white sesame seeds

1½ cups (4 oz/125 g) very finely shredded kale

1½ cups (4 oz/125 g) very finely shredded savoy or napa cabbage

½ bunch fresh cilantro, roughly chopped

¼ avocado, peeled and cut into large chunks

FOR THE DRESSING

¼ cup (2 fl oz/60 ml) cold-pressed flax oil

¼ cup (2 fl oz/60 ml) cold-pressed sesame oil

¼ cup (2 fl oz/60 ml) rice vinegar

1 tablespoon organic, gluten-free shoyu soy sauce, such as Eden organic

1 tablespoon raw almond butter

½-inch (12-mm) knob fresh ginger

½ clove garlic, passed through a garlic press

1 tablespoon coconut palm sugar (optional)

¼ cup (¼ oz/7 g) micro sprouts

2 radishes, cut in half lengthwise

1 sheet raw nori, about 7 by 8 inches (18 by 20 cm), torn into small pieces

To make the salad, put the carrots in a bowl, add the black sesame seeds and 1 tablespoon of the rice vinegar, and toss well; set aside. In another bowl, toss the purple cabbage with the white sesame seeds and 1 tablespoon rice vinegar and set aside.

Put the kale and savoy cabbage in a large bowl. Set aside ¼ cup (⅓ oz/10 g) of the cilantro and add the rest along with the avocado to the bowl. Toss to mix well.

To make the dressing, in a blender, combine the flax and sesame oils, rice vinegar, shoyu, almond butter, ginger, garlic, coconut sugar, if using, and reserved cilantro and blend until smooth.

Drizzle 2–3 tablespoons of the dressing, or to taste, over the salad and toss to coat evenly. Transfer the salad to a plate. Arrange the carrot mixture on the edge of the salad, then arrange the purple cabbage mixture next to the carrots. Arrange the sprouts and radishes in piles on the other side of the carrots. Tear the nori into small pieces and sprinkle over the salad. (If you like, you can also toss all the ingredients together.) Serve right away.

Prepare your medicinal spa bath

Tonight you're going to try a vinegar bath. You may already know that vinegar is wonder stuff: its natural astringency is ideal for everything from cleaning the scalp to cleaning a kitchen countertop. When you add vinegar to a bath, it helps make the body more alkaline by clearing acidity. To help mask the strong smell of the vinegar, I've chosen rosemary essential oil. I also like rosemary oil for its antioxidant benefits and because it can enhance circulation. As always, it's up to you whether or not you choose to add the aromatherapeutic component.

CIDER VINEGAR BATH

3–3½ cups (24–28 fl oz/750–875 ml) cider vinegar
8 drops rosemary essential oil (optional)

To make your bath, fill the tub with the hottest water you can stand and add the vinegar, swirling it around to be sure it is evenly distributed. Add your fragrance drops, if using, under running water. Soak in the tub for 20 minutes.

Write in your journal

Tonight, write about how you're feeling as compared to yesterday. Do you feel empowered? Weak? Inspired? Tired? Record your feelings about being halfway through the cleanse and how it has affected you physically and mentally. Are you missing your normal patterns and foods? Are you having cravings? Are there any aspects of this program you'd like to continue after the four days are over? Make notes on all of it. As your body lets go of weight and physical cravings, ask yourself what emotional patterns you plan to also let go.

OPTIONAL
Enjoy a before-bed treat

Bring a cup of the Alkalizing Mineral Broth that you made on Day 1 (PAGE 64) to a boil, let cool slightly, and stir in 1 teaspoon miso. Sip slowly.

OPTIONAL
Practice a pre-sleep meditation

Follow the instructions on page 71 to complete tonight's meditation. After you are finished with the waterfall imagery and are feeling clean and clear, scan your body, mind, and spirit and ask yourself if there are any hidden blocks, old patterns, or negativity that are holding you back from being the vibrant, healthy person you were born to be. If you detect any of the above, imagine breathing in white light (which represents love) and exhaling the blockage or negativity. Repeat this process until you feel you have cleared it, or at least begin the process of letting it go. Acknowledge the work you are doing and praise yourself for giving yourself this gift. End the meditation by sending yourself a big dose of loving thoughts.

A therapeutic bath
each night of the
cleanse is a great way
to pamper yourself

LEFT TO RIGHT

Raw Avocado-Carrot Soup, Dandelion Liver Tonic, Vital Citrus Juice, Zucchini Pasta with Tomato Sauce and Pine Nut–Hemp Pesto, Alkalizing Mineral Broth

CLEANSE / **DAY 3** /

/ DAY **1** /

/ DAY **2** /

/ DAY **3** /

/ DAY **4** /

CLEANSE / DAY 3 /

Are you getting into the swing of this? By the third day, I'm usually beginning to hit my cleansing stride, though others say it takes them four. At this point, I'm typically feeling lighter and more focused and I'm thinking, "I can do this for as long as I want!" That may be a stretch for some of you, and that's okay. Feeling tired, cranky, headachy, and fighting cravings is all part of the deal. If you're dependent on caffeine, sugar, alcohol, meat, and dairy, or on any combination of those, you may be experiencing some withdrawal symptoms. Just keep at it and know you're giving your body a much-deserved break.

Make your gratitude list

Once again, write down the things that you are grateful for. Think about what new things are coming up for you since the first two days of the cleanse and note others that remain constant. Really try to feel the gratitude and imagine rays of it filling the sky above you.

Drink warm lemon water

Follow the instructions on page 61 to make your lemon water. Sip slowly before you do anything else.

Dry brush your skin and shower

Follow the instructions on page 61 to dry brush your skin. Follow with a warm shower and an optional cool rinse.

Make your green juice

You're now on your third day, so you're able to build up the detoxification methods at this point. I will come clean and admit that this green juice is pretty bitter. It's also exceptionally powerful and very good for you. Even if you decide you'll never want to drink this one again, give it a try now. You may decide to add a green juice every day and choose a sweeter one from the recipes on pages 130–137. That's great. But before you do, I want you to have the experience of all kinds of juices with healthful properties. And you may surprise yourself. You may decide you like it.

DANDELION LIVER TONIC

For the best results, always juice leafy greens between any dense vegetables, such as the celery, carrots, and cucumber here.

> 4 celery ribs
> 1–2 cups (1–2 oz/30–60 g) spinach leaves
> 2 kale leaves
> ¼ bunch dandelion greens
> ¼ bunch fresh flat-leaf parsley
> 2 carrots
> 1 cucumber

Cut the vegetables as needed into pieces that will fit into the chute of your extraction juicer. Then, following the manufacturer's instructions, juice all of the ingredients in the order given. Pour into a tall glass.

Make your breakfast

Instead of solid food today, we are going to take advantage of the Alkalizing Mineral Broth for its soothing, probiotic properties. Instead of your usual small cup, enjoy a big, warm bowl of the mineral broth with 1 tablespoon of miso stirred in. We're consuming broth instead of solid food at this point in the cleanse in order to give your GI tract a break. In traditional Chinese medicine, warmth supports and strengthens the spleen and stomach, which both aids digestion as well as ensures optimal absorption of nutrients to boost energy levels.

Select a morning activity

Choose one of the activities on pages 97–99 for this morning.

Make your lunch

Today, you will make a raw soup. Now, some of you may be recoiling at my use of the word raw, but trust me when I say that raw doesn't have to mean unappetizing. Every recipe I create starts with the aim to make something that tastes good (yes, I know that some of you will argue with me about my unsweetened green juices), and a well-balanced raw soup with great flavor, some healthy fats, and the right amount of herbs or spices can stand up to any standard soup recipe in taste and texture. This soup proves that statement to be true.

> If any of the recipes on this day don't appeal to you, try any green-based juice on pages 130–137; the Bloody Great (PAGE 134) instead of the citrus juice; or any salad from pages 149–153 in place of the zucchini pasta.

RAW AVOCADO-CARROT SOUP

Soothing and flavorful, this soup gets its hefty dose of omega-3s and its rich, thick texture from the avocado, its vitamin A from the carrot juice, and its anti-inflammatory power from the ginger and mint.

- 1 avocado, halved, pitted, and peeled
- 1 cup fresh carrot juice (from 6 jumbo or 12 small carrots)
- 1 cup (1 oz/30 g) spinach leaves
- 1-inch (2.5-cm) knob fresh ginger, coarsely chopped
- 1 tablespoon fresh mint leaves
- 2 tablespoons fresh lemon juice
- 1 teaspoon sea salt
- ¼ jalapeño chile (optional)

In a blender, combine the avocado, carrot juice, spinach, ginger, mint, lemon juice, salt, and the chile, if you want a spicy flavor, and blend on high speed until smooth. Pour into a bowl and enjoy at room temperature.

Enjoy an afternoon juice

An hour or so after your soup lunch, try this refreshing citrus blend.

VITAL CITRUS JUICE

Rich in vitamins C and A, this juice is perfect when your immune system needs a boost or you have a cold.

- 1 grapefruit, peeled
- 2 oranges, peeled
- 1 lemon, peeled
- 2 carrots
- 2-inch (5-cm) knob fresh turmeric
- ¼ bunch fresh cilantro

Cut the fruits and carrots as needed into pieces that will fit into the chute of your extraction juicer. Then, following the manufacturer's instructions, juice all of the ingredients in the order given. Pour into a tall glass.

Select an afternoon activity

Choose one of the optional activities on pages 97–99 to do this afternoon. If it were me, I'd go out into nature and take a long, semi-vigorous hike, taking a break from my mobile phone, computer, and social media.

Enjoy an afternoon snack

Bring a cup of the Alkalizing Mineral Broth that you made on Day 1 (PAGE 64) to a boil, let cool slightly, and stir in 1 teaspoon miso. Sip slowly.

Make your dinner

Some people think the presence of hemp on a menu is funny. It seems so, well, hippie, doesn't it? But for those of us in the health community, hemp is a prized nutrition source that offers a range of benefits from digestive regulation to cardiovascular health. And the taste has a sweet, pleasing, cheeselike flavor.

ZUCCHINI PASTA WITH TOMATO SAUCE AND PINE NUT–HEMP PESTO

The spiral-sliced zucchini in this recipe mimics the texture of real pasta without the carbs and satisfies a craving for a flavorful, Italian-style meal. If you don't have a spiral slicer, you can use a mandoline to create thin zucchini ribbons, but you won't get the same spaghetti-like texture. These are generous portions of tomato sauce and pesto, but you can refrigerate or freeze them to enjoy after your cleanse.

> 3 zucchini, each 6–7 inches (15–18 cm) long
>
> FOR THE TOMATO SAUCE
> 2 cups (6 oz/185 g) dry-packed sun-dried tomatoes, soaked in 3 cups (24 fl oz/750 ml) water for 5 hours and drained, with water reserved
>
> 7 fresh basil leaves
>
> 1 clove garlic, minced
>
> ¼ cup (2 fl oz/60 ml) extra-virgin olive oil
>
> 1 teaspoon sea salt

FOR THE PESTO
3 cups (3 oz/90 g) fresh basil leaves
¼ cup (1¼ oz/35 g) pine nuts
¼ cup (1¼ oz/35 g) shelled hemp seeds
1 large clove garlic, coarsely chopped
½ cup (4 fl oz/125 ml) extra-virgin olive oil
1 teaspoon sea salt

Using a spiral vegetable cutter, cut the zucchini into noodles and put them in a colander to drain off any moisture while you make the tomato sauce and pesto.

To make the tomato sauce, in a blender, combine the soaked tomatoes, 2 cups (16 fl oz/500 ml) of the soaking water, the basil, garlic, oil, and salt and process until smooth. If the sauce seems too thick, add more of the soaking water until a good consistency is achieved.

To make the pesto, in a food processor, combine the basil, pine nuts, hemp seeds, garlic, oil, and salt and process until well blended but still a bit chunky.

You can eat the zucchini noodles at room temperature, or you can warm them slightly in a frying pan over low heat for about 1 minute. Transfer the noodles to an individual serving bowl or plate, top with sauce to your taste (I like to smother them), and toss to mix well. Top with a dollop of the pesto.

Transfer any remaining sauce or pesto to separate airtight containers and refrigerate for 3–4 days.

Prepare your medicinal spa bath

Tonight you will be slipping into a hot bath that combines salt, baking soda, and vinegar. Does that formulation sound familiar? It should, as it is a hybrid of the two baths you've taken over the past two nights. And that means it gives you both sets of benefits. For this bath, I'm recommending lavender as your aromatherapeutic oil, both for its pleasant fragrance and its incredible relaxing properties. You're going to sleep like a baby after this bath.

Ingredients for the
Salt, Soda, and
Vinegar Bath

/ DAY **3** /

Sipping Alkalizing Mineral Broth is an essential part of your four-day retreat

½ cup (3¾ oz/115 g) sea salt or Himalayan pink salt

½ cup (3½ oz/105 g) aluminum-free baking soda

¼ cup (2 oz/60 g) Epsom salts

¼ cup (2 fl oz/60 ml) cider vinegar

12 drops lavender essential oil (optional)

To make your bath, fill the tub with the hottest water you can stand, add the salt, baking soda, Epsom salts, and vinegar, and swirl the water around to be sure all the granules dissolve and the vinegar is evenly distributed. Add your fragrance drops, if using, under running water. Soak in the tub for 20 minutes.

Write in your journal

Have any new insights occurred to you during your cleanse? Do you have fresh resolve to accomplish your goals? Do you think you could cleanse for even longer than four days? Tomorrow is your final day, so take stock in how it feels to have come this far. Ask yourself: what are you willing to change or to let go? What actions will you take?

Tonight, make a list of all the actions you need to take to support letting go of the things that are getting in your way. If you need to write down pros and cons, please do so. For example, the pros of eating white flour and sugar are that they taste great. The cons of eating these ingredients are that they make me tired, feel sluggish, and promote an unhealthy body.

OPTIONAL
Enjoy a before-bed treat

Bring a cup of the Alkalizing Mineral Broth that you made on Day 1 (PAGE 64) to a boil, let cool slightly, and stir in 1 teaspoon miso. Sip slowly.

OPTIONAL
Practice a pre-sleep meditation

Follow the instructions on page 71 to complete tonight's meditation.

Love is what makes us feel whole and connected in life. In every situation you have a choice to either love or fear. Love is surrender and learning through life's difficulties. Fear is resistance and feeling like a victim in difficult situations, or blaming others rather than learning and moving forward. The feelings of love help to balance the brain and nervous system. Tonight, at the end of the waterfall meditation, focus on self love. Imagine pure love around your heart in a golden light. Expand the love to fill your lungs and chest, up to your head and down to your feet. Imagine this golden light shooting out through the front and back of your heart. Focus on the notion that love is your birthright and is within you always.

To end the meditation, take a few deep breaths and, when you feel ready, slowly open your eyes.

LEFT TO RIGHT
Sunflower Sprout
and Carrot Juice,
Dandelion Liver Tonic,
Alkalizing Mineral
Broth, Mediterranean
Mix Salad, Tummy
Lover Juice

CLEANSE / DAY 4 /

Can you believe it? It's the last day of the cleanse. Some of you are thinking, "I want more. I could do this for a week!" If you are among them, more power to you. You've learned the elements that go into each day, and discovered a number of great recipes from which you can pick if you decide to continue. On the other hand, you may be thinking you're ready to slowly reenter your regular routine, and that's great too. When you do, you'll be making better choices and coming at life with a new degree of insight.

Make your gratitude list

As you write down the things for which you are grateful for the final time during this cleanse, think about how your perspective has changed from the first day to now. Reflect on how this practice is a great way to start the day and consider incorporating it into your daily life.

Drink warm lemon water

Follow the instructions on page 61 to make your lemon water. Sip slowly before you do anything else.

Dry brush your skin and shower

Follow the instructions on page 61 to dry brush your skin. Follow with a warm shower and an optional cool rinse.

Make your green juice

Make the Good Morning Green Juice (PAGE 74) that you enjoyed on Day 2 of your cleanse.

Make your breakfast

Bring enough of the Alkalizing Mineral Broth that you made on Day 1 (PAGE 64) for a large bowl to a boil. Let it cool slightly, and stir in 1 tablespoon miso. Sip slowly.

Select a morning activity

Choose one of the optional activities on pages 97–99 to do this morning.

Make your lunch

Today's lunch is a simple juice that you'll want to sip even when you are not on a cleanse. It is your last day of the program, so you will be flushing your system with more juice and less solid food than on other days.

SUNFLOWER SPROUT AND CARROT JUICE

Rich in zinc, antioxidants, and vitamins A and B, this sunny blend is a refreshing treat. If you can't find sunflower sprouts, substitute another type of sprouts like broccoli or alfalfa.

> 2–3 cups (4–6 oz/125–185 g) sunflower sprouts
> 5 or 6 carrots
> 2 lemons, peeled

Cut the carrots and lemons as needed into pieces that will fit into the chute of your extraction juicer. Then, following the manufacturer's instructions, juice all of the ingredients in the order given. Pour into a tall glass.

Greet every morning of your cleanse
with system-revving lemon water

Gratitude lists are an important part of resetting your intentions

Enjoy an afternoon juice break

About 2 hours after lunch, make this juice and sip it while you sit in your favorite spot. This juice supports gastrointestinal health. Having a strong digestive system is the foundation of overall vitality. The ability to assimilate nutrients through the stomach and intestines is essential to overall health, making this juice a great fortifier for your final cleanse day.

TUMMY LOVER JUICE

This is a great juice to add to your repertoire, especially if you're prone to an upset tummy or to acid reflux. It is the go-to juice for all stomach issues.

- 2 cups (6 oz/180 g) chopped purple cabbage
- 1-inch (2.5-cm) knob fresh ginger
- 2 Granny Smith apples
- ½ fennel bulb
- 2 lemons, peeled
- ¼ cup (2 fl oz/60 ml) filtered water, if needed

Cut the apples, fennel, and lemons as needed into pieces that will fit into the chute of your extraction juicer. Then, following the manufacturer's instructions, juice the cabbage, ginger, apples, fennel, and lemons, in that order. If the juice volume seems low, pour the water through the juicer. Pour the juice into a tall glass.

Select an afternoon activity

Choose one of the optional activities on pages 97–99 to do this afternoon.

If the recipes for today don't appeal to you, substitute the Beetnik (PAGE 130) or Skin Beautiful juice (PAGE 133) for Sunflower Sprout and Carrot Juice; or substitute Apple Wheatgrass Blast (PAGE 137) or Sweet Breath Juice (PAGE 138) for the Tummy Lover Juice.

Enjoy an afternoon snack

Bring a cup of the Alkalizing Mineral Broth that you made on Day 1 (PAGE 64) to a boil, let cool slightly, and stir in 1 teaspoon miso. Sip slowly.

Make your dinner

I like Middle Eastern food. If you do too, you will enjoy this celebratory salad.

MEDITERRANEAN MIX SALAD

Look for the sprouted chickpeas in your local health food store. If you can't find them, add some avocado to the salad instead.

- 3 cups (4½ oz/140 g) chopped romaine lettuce
- ¼ cup (1½ oz/45 g) cherry tomatoes, halved
- ¼ cup (1¾ oz/50 g) sprouted raw chickpeas
- ¼ cucumber, halved, seeded, and cut into ½-inch (12-mm) pieces
- 1 tablespoon coarsely chopped fresh mint
- ½ clove garlic, passed through a garlic press
- ¼ teaspoon sea salt
- 1 tablespoon cold-pressed extra-virgin olive oil
- 1 teaspoon cold-pressed flax oil
- 1 tablespoon cider vinegar

Put the romaine lettuce, tomatoes, chickpeas, cucumber, and mint in a bowl and toss to mix well. Sprinkle with the garlic and salt, drizzle evenly with the oils and vinegar, and toss again.

Prepare your medicinal spa bath

Your final medicinal bath combines hydrogen peroxide and ginger, the former a serious detoxifier (oxygenating) and the latter a powerful anti-inflammatory agent. Some people find this bath intense, meaning that they feel depleted afterward. To me, that's a sign of serious relaxation and detoxification. It should promote an excellent night's sleep.

HYDROGEN PEROXIDE AND GINGER BATH

6 cups (48 fl oz/1.5 l) hydrogen peroxide

⅔ cup (2 oz/60 g) ground ginger

6 drops peppermint essential oil (optional)

To make your bath, fill the tub with the hottest water you can stand, add the hydrogen peroxide and ginger, and swirl the water around to be sure they are evenly distributed. Add the essential oil, if using. Soak in the tub for 20 minutes.

Perform the fire ceremony

I like to close a cleanse with an ancient ritual that's used across many cultures to signal renewal and purification. Because fire transforms something tangible into something unseen, it is a fitting symbol of change. I also like the dramatic, ceremonial aspect of it. Tonight, this ritual will take the place of—and serve as the culmination of—your journal writing.

At the beginning of the cleanse, you focused on your intention and what you wanted to let go of in your life. Now is the time to give yourself permission to release those things. If you have not done so already, with a strong intention, write down whatever negative energy, emotions, or memories you long to let go. Take a moment to think about the fact that you're consciously doing away with these aspects and then burn the paper in a fireplace, fire pit, or even over a candle. (For those who think this feels like a spell or witchcraft, it's not. It's simply a physical act that symbolizes your letting go.) When you burn the paper and watch it vanish to nothing, it's a potent way of enacting your desire. Seeing those negative aspects reduced to ash is an exercise in affirmation. When you throw the paper into the fire, it's a powerful metaphor for releasing whatever is holding you back in your

life. Take a moment to reflect on the gratitude you feel for completing the cleanse and having the courage to change your life.

As a complementary ritual, you may choose to write the positive affirmations that represent the release of negativity. For example, if your negative statement says something like, "I want to let go of feeling tired, unhealthy, and unhappy all the time," your affirmation might read, "I am vibrant and healthy. I enjoy life to the fullest." Keep these affirmations somewhere you can see them and reflect on them daily—you can even say them aloud, an exercise in personal empowerment.

Remember that this cleanse wasn't a stand-alone act. It's meant to kickstart a whole new healthy lifestyle. You can use this knowledge for the rest of your life. For example, if you have an indulgent night or weekend, drink some green juice during the week or try a whole day of clean eating. You can also share the power of what you have learned with friends and family.

OPTIONAL
Enjoy a before-bed treat

Bring a cup of the Alkalizing Mineral Broth that you made on Day 1 (PAGE 64) to a boil, let cool slightly, and stir in 1 teaspoon miso. Sip slowly.

OPTIONAL
Practice a pre-sleep meditation

Follow the instructions on page 71 to complete tonight's meditation. Add in one of your favorite extensions of the practice from days 2, 3, or 4.

Meditating during your cleanse (or anytime)
has a calming, grounding effect

OPTIONAL ACTIVITIES TO COMPLEMENT YOUR CLEANSE

When I lead cleanse retreats, I integrate practices like acupuncture and light yoga and also provide access to an infrared sauna. When you're doing your cleanse at home, you can choose which, if any, additional practices you want to try. Some of these activities can be done at your house, while others will involve a trip to a gym or a massage spa. Each one of these options is beneficial in its own right, but none of them is mandatory in completing a cleanse. They simply serve to further detox, relax, and stimulate healing.

SAUNA /

Saunas have been used in traditional Chinese medicine for centuries. They are seen as a way to promote circulation of qi (energy) and blood, encourage sweating, and stimulate the immune system. Saunas also release toxins from the body through sweating and can promote deep relaxation while balancing the physical body. They are, however, contraindicated for people with yin deficiency or weak constitutions, or for the elderly and young children.

You may discover that you also have access to an infrared sauna, which is sort of a supercharged sauna that produces infrared light that is absorbed by the skin in the form of radiant heat. The heat emitted by an infrared sauna is cooler than the heat produced in a conventional sauna, but it travels more deeply into the body. That means that it detoxifies at a deeper level than what is possible in a conventional sauna, so that it creates a more vigorous sweat and thus more effectively releases heavy metals and other toxins. Infrared saunas are often prescribed by healthcare practitioners for ridding the body of heavy metals from dental work, or to counteract a high mercury content detected in the system.

MASSAGE /

Many people regard a massage as a pampering treat, but in Chinese medicine, massage, or *tui na*, is also an important healing tool that complements acupuncture, cupping (SEE PAGE 98), and herbal and diet therapy. It is used to promote circulation, reduce pain, and relax the nervous system. If it is within your budget, I recommend that you treat yourself to a deep massage at some point—or points, if you are lucky—during the course of the four-day cleanse.

YOGA /

Yoga supports the healthy flow of energy by releasing stuck emotions and optimizing healthy energy flow to the meridians. If yoga appeals to you, I recommend that you attend a yoga class or classes over the course of the cleanse during your midmorning or afternoon activity time. Of course, if you're an experienced yogi, you can follow your own practice at home.

WALKING MEDITATION /

Many people are aware of seated meditation, but walking is another way to experience the calming, grounding effects of a meditation practice. Derived from Buddhist tradition, walking meditation is simply that: the act of mindfully moving through space while actively becoming aware of your surroundings. While Buddhist monks often practice walking meditation using artful ground paths or labyrinths, you can try walking meditation anywhere. I recommend a natural space, rather than an urban one—somewhere you can focus on your surroundings in a peaceful way. Choose a park or beach nearby and just plan to walk, slowly and with small steps, for 20 minutes or so. While you do, notice everything from the sensation in your body to the sun on your face. Activate the senses to become aware of the birdsong, the waves, or the rustle of leaves. This practice is centering, but also incredibly invigorating. Taking notice of the sensory elements all around us can inspire deep wonder and gratitude at the simple beauty we are often too distracted to notice or enjoy.

FOOT BATH /

The liver, gall bladder, kidney, spleen, and stomach meridians flow to or from the feet. By soaking your feet in hot water, you will open the circulation in these meridians throughout your body. You can use your bathtub, purchase a tub specifically designed for foot baths, or even use a large bowl or bucket.

To create your foot bath, fill the bath with the hottest water possible, add fresh ginger slices and dandelion greens, and let steep for 10 minutes. (The amount of ginger slices and dandelion greens depends on the size of the foot bath; plan on about 1 cup (4 oz/125 g) chopped ginger and 1 bunch dandelion greens for every 4 qt (4 l) water.) Once the water cools a bit, soak your feet for 20 minutes. This is especially effective for combating the symptoms of colds and flu.

ACUPUNCTURE /

Acupuncture is the primary mode of treatment in traditional Chinese medicine. This ancient practice is used to move energy by stimulating qi, and to tap into the meridians and organs that need healing attention. Using needles that are as fine as a hair, an acupuncturist inserts the needles, varying their depth, into the skin at a series of specific points on the body to treat a patient's particular ailment or constitution. For many Westerners, the idea of having needle treatment sounds scary and painful, but in fact, the insertion of an acupuncture needle is almost undetectable. What is detectable is the sensation in the body once the needles are inserted. Depending on your constitution, you may feel a tingle, a dull ache, a kind of electrical charge, or just deep relaxation.

CUPPING AND MOXIBUSTION /

Cupping is a traditional Chinese therapy that uses glass cups and heat to create suction to unblock stuck or stagnant energy. It helps to relax muscles and stimulate qi energy flow. Cupping can be used on specific acupuncture points for colds, flu, high blood pressure, or pain. Some practitioners even use it for weight loss and to reduce cellulite. Moxibustion employs the herb mugwort, which is ignited and then applied to areas of the body, sometimes with an acupuncture needle, where the qi is not moving properly. The mugwort will stimulate energy movement in the area.

TONGUE SCRAPING /

Looking at the tongue is one of the primary methods of diagnosis in Chinese medicine. The color, size, and coating of the tongue impart insight about the internal health of the body. Using a specialized tongue cleaner to scrape your tongue the first thing in the morning removes bacteria and can help to freshen your breath. Do not scrape your tongue before seeing your Chinese medicine practitioner, however, or he or she will be unable to diagnose you accurately. Look for tongue cleaners at a health food store.

CASTOR OIL PACK /

Castor oil has long been used to the heal the body in many parts of the world, such as ancient Egypt, India, China, Persia, Africa, Greece, and Rome. Records show it was also used in the early Middle Ages in Europe and in the Americas. It is known to be effective for many types of pain, liver and gallbladder stimulation and cleansing, lymphatic circulation, digestive problems, lacerations, skin disorders such as eczema or psoriasis, menopause symptoms, boosting the immune system, softening the skin, and much more.

Castor oil packs are tools that I've used in my practice with great results. Castor oil is truly one of the earth's most versatile healing gifts—and it's easy to use, especially in the form of a pack, which is simply flannel fabric soaked with the oil, placed on the area to be treated, and then covered with a heating pad. The heat opens the skin's pores and encourages the oil to enter the body through them. Here is what you will need to assemble the pack, followed by directions for putting it together and then applying it.

CASTOR OIL PACK

- Large piece of certified organic natural beige cotton flannel, at least 30 by 36 inches (76 by 90 cm)
- Plastic wrap or a plastic trash bag
- 1 bottle (4 fl oz/125 ml) 100 percent virgin cold-pressed castor oil
- Heating pad
- Cotton bath towel (optional)

Fold or cut the flannel to create a triple-thickness pack. The pack should be large enough to cover the area to be treated. For example, to use the pack on your abdomen, it should measure 10 inches (25 cm) long by 8 inches (20 cm) wide. The packs can be smaller or slightly larger (up to 12 by 10 inches/30 by 25 cm). A typical pack measures 8 by 6 inches (20 by 15 cm).

Cut a sheet of plastic wrap so it is somewhat larger than the flannel pack. The plastic wrap is used to prevent the heating pad from getting oily or stained by the castor oil. A plastic trash bag can also be used, but it is usually best to avoid plastic grocery bags, as they are often printed on one side with ink, which can break down and spread when it comes in contact with the castor oil.

Place the flannel pack on top of the plastic sheet, then evenly saturate the cloth with 3–4 tablespoons castor oil. The cloth should be wet but not dripping. Place the saturated cloth directly on the skin, with the plastic sheet on top. The plastic must cover the entire exterior of the saturated flannel to avoid staining the heating pad.

Now, place the heating pad on top of the plastic sheet and turn on the pad to either a low or a medium setting, or higher if it is comfortable. If you like, place the bath towel over the heating pad to help hold in the heat. The heat will promote absorption, increase circulation, and help the body to relax. Leave the castor oil pack in place for 30–60 minutes.

Once the treatment is finished, remove the castor oil pack and cleanse the skin with a dampened washcloth and liquid soap. Washing the area well helps clear away the acidic toxins that have been drawn out of the body during the treatment and prevents their reabsorption.

Each cotton flannel pack must be used only once and then discarded. That's because it has absorbed toxins and waste products during the treatment. Do not attempt to wash the pack and reuse it.

COLONICS /

For those of you feeling a little more adventurous in your cleanse, you can opt to try a colonic, a treatment designed to move blocked material in the colon by releasing warm water into the bowels through a light-pressured hose. I particularly recommend a colonic, also known as colonic hydrotherapy, colon irrigation, or home enema, for people with chronic constipation. I don't recommend long-term treatment, but one to three treatments can make you feel lighter and unblocked, especially during a cleanse. There are detox clinics that specialize in colonics. Colonic treatments can be pricey. A less costly alternative is to purchase an enema kit from your local drugstore and administer an enema at home. If you go that route, follow the instructions to the letter. Be sure to consult a trusted health practitioner before trying colonics or at-home enemas.

AFTER YOUR CLEANSE

You did it! Hopefully you are feeling more energized than before and your skin is glowing and clear. I encourage you to keep incorporating the healthy principles you learned over the last 4 days into your life. If you feel up to it, you can keep going on the cleanse for a few more days. There are plenty of delicious recipes on pages 124–168 to keep you inspired, Or, simply incorporate the recipes as you like into your daily meals. Imagine what you'd feel like if you ate like this all the time? Even just reducing the number of "unhealthy days" in your life will make a big difference. For those of you with superbusy schedules, there are lots of ways to stay healthy, such as committing to eating clean 1–3 days per week to keep you on track. Whatever method you choose, try to limit your intake of inflammatory foods for optimal health. Also, make an effort to keep the healthy eating and thought patterns a part of your lifestyle.

On the day after you have completed your cleanse, you don't want to shock your system by jumping right back into a heavy diet. Take it easy on your body as you reacclimate to your routine. Start your day with a green juice and choose a breakfast such as the Raw Apple Granola with Almond Crème (PAGE 63) or Antioxidant Green Smoothie (PAGE 75) or one of the recipes on pages 124–168. You'll find a number of wonderful options from which to choose. The rest of day, try to eat fruits and vegetables and sip mineral broth, if you still have some on hand. Eat clean foods for the next three to five days, as you did in the lead-up to the cleanse. Also, to cut down on overall sugar consumption, try to incorporate healthful low-glycemic foods into your diet as a lifestyle change.

Foods you can eat freely

○ Fruits and vegetables, especially those with dark pigments like kale and other dark leafy greens, tomatoes, red bell peppers, purple cabbage, blueberries, and cranberries

○ Soaked nuts (SEE PAGE 168) and seeds in small quantities

○ Unfiltered cold-pressed flaxseed, olive, sesame, sunflower, almond, coconut, hemp, macadamia nut, and grapeseed oil

○ All green juices, vegetable juices, and diluted fruit juices (half fruit juice and half filtered water)

○ Antioxidant-rich superfoods, such as açai, cacao, goji berries, spirulina, blueberries, maca, wheatgrass, and hemp

○ Fermented foods like raw sauerkraut, kefir, and miso to support a healthy gut and immune system

Think about what you are going to eat and then ask yourself whether your choices cleanse your body or clog your body. Fresh organic vegetables are excellent detoxifiers. Most fruits are filled with water, which helps to cleanse and hydrate the body. Think salads, lightly steamed vegetables, juices, and soups.

Try to remove processed foods completely from your diet. I'm talking about packaged foods like crackers, cookies, chips, muffins, fast foods, and canned foods. These foods often include unhealthy oils, lard, trans fats, white sugar, and white flour, which tend to promote inflammation in the body.

Additional foods to remove from your diet or to eat only in small quantities include dairy, meat, alcohol, and grains, especially gluten-containing grains such as all varieties of wheat, barley, and rye. All grains and carbohydrates will slow your cleansing process, so the more you eat, the slower you'll cleanse. This is because they don't have the enzymes found in raw fruits and vegetables, so it takes longer for your body to digest them.

One of the worst things that you can do to clog your body is overeat. Even if you are eating healthy foods, overeating puts a huge strain on the digestive process and burdens the whole GI tract. Please try and eat smaller meals. I promise that you will feel lighter and have much more energy. The less you eat, the more your body responds by turning on the antiaging (anti-inflammatory and antidiabetic) genes, as long as you are eating whole foods, that is, fresh foods that are raw or only lightly altered from their living state.

Maintenance Programs

Often after completing a cleanse, people decide that they love the way they felt when they finished, and even though they can't eat that way every day, they like to integrate a modified cleanse program into their regular routine. Here are the easiest ways to do that.

ONE DAY A WEEK / Whether you've completed a short or a long cleanse, it's easy to get stuck in old patterns, but a one-day maintenance cleanse keeps you in the right frame of mind. It's enough to interrupt cravings for sugar and flour, and it's a smart way to counteract the ever-present toxins from pollution and foods. A once-weekly cleanse promotes optimum health and antiaging.

TWO DAYS A WEEK / Cleanse two days a week and you'll experience all of the benefits described in the one-day cleanse (above), plus a stronger resolve to stay healthy and mindful.

EVERY DAY / You may decide to start eating clean foods every day once your cleanse ends. Or, you can keep up your daily juice consumption using any of the recipes in the book while you reintroduce food. This gives you all the nutrients you need for optimal health and helps to fill you up so you require less solid food. For people trying to lose weight or address general health issues, this option supports overall well-being. With juices as a part of your daily intake, you are likely to make better choices in the kitchen, reaching for a healthful alternative to junk food.

FOOD AS MEDICINE

Let food be thy medicine and medicine be thy food.

—Hippocrates, the father of Western Medicine, 460-377 BC

As you can see by this quote, the idea of using food to prevent and balance overall health is not a new idea. In fact, it is the basis of many ancient healing systems. Everything we put into our bodies creates a chemical reaction. I encourage you to adopt a new way of looking at food and eating foods that truly nourish your body.

Once you start to learn the medicinal values of food, you have the power to be more healthy and share what you have learned with friends and family.

This section consists of two parts. First, I provide a glossary of ingredients that are especially helpful for cleanses and for general health. Second, I include a guide to treating specific ailments with specific foods, according to the principles of TCM. This is the same information that I would share with you if you came to see me in person.

I'd like to share an anecdote that illustrates how food can act as medicine. It is the story of a woman named Mara, who serves as an example of the powerful healing that eating the right foods can offer.

MARA Mara struggled for ten years with debilitating headaches and anxiety. She had seen all of the top neurological doctors, Western and Eastern, and they had not been able to pinpoint her issue. She had endured hospital stays and taken many pain medications. When she finally came to me and explained her neurological history, I recommended an anti-inflammatory regimen and a detox because of the many medications she had taken, both of which she followed. Mara started tracking her progress. Her neurologist had always pushed her—after pain cycles and hospital stays—to do colon and liver cleanses. I added dandelion, burdock, and turmeric to that prescription, administered acupuncture treatments, proposed she eliminate gluten, and suggested dietary supplements. The first thing that Mara's tracking showed was that her recovery after a pain cycle was far shorter than it had been the past. That meant that she was able to return to her regular routine much sooner. The second thing the tracking revealed was that when she stuck to her diet plan, the time between headaches was much longer. Mara is healthy and health-minded—she owns a Pilates studio—but when she skips the recommended dietary ingredients, she loses energy, doesn't sleep well, and gets more headaches. That has made drinking healthful juices a way of life for the rest of her life. Even Mara's neurologist says it makes perfect sense. Western medicine has not figured out what triggers cause her muscles to inflame and spasm, but natural anti-inflammatories have calmed Mara's muscle tension and an intense liver detox after a pain cycle now ensures a quicker recovery.

Glossary of Healthful Properties of Common Foods

This list contains the most common and hardworking ingredients in my juices and dishes. These foods are easily found in most health food stores. My goal is to empower you to understand the medicinal benefits of what is included here, so you can use them in your everyday routine. For more information on the energetic properties of each type of food, turn to the chart on page 117. On page 116, you'll find a list of common ailments and foods that can be used to treat them, an alternative approach to some of the same information.

APPLE / Those proverbial doctors must have been right when they said, "An apple a day keeps the doctor away." Apples contain sweet health-supporting phytochemicals that may prevent disease and protect your body temple, plus they contain flavonoids, which support lowering inflammation and regulating the immune system. You may be surprised to learn that apple juice also contains soluble and insoluble fiber to help lower cholesterol and scrub out accumulated waste from the intestines. Eating apples is a great way to fight hunger pangs and keep blood sugar balanced, especially when combined with a handful of raw or soaked almonds. Apple juice is good for tonifying the qi.

Apple juice is good
for tonifying the qi.

苹果

APPLE

Apples contain sweet
health-supporting
phytochemicals that
may prevent disease.

甘藍菜 CABBAGE

in TCM, cabbage juice is prescribed for treating stomach ailments.

Cabbage juice contains more vitamin C than oranges and is believed to inhibit certain types of cancer.

BEET / This popular taproot of the vegetable kingdom carries major clout in the world of good health. Its bright red juice is rich in phytonutrients called betalains, which have been shown to provide antioxidant, anti-inflammatory, and detoxification support. Rich in nitrogen, beets have the ability to reduce high blood pressure and oxygenate the blood for energy. In traditional Chinese medicine, beets are used to build the blood, support the heart, calm the spirit, lubricate the intestines, and cleanse the liver to eliminate such syndromes as irritability, anxiety, constipation, and intoxication from drugs or alcohol.

BURDOCK / Known as a blood purifier, burdock root is used in Ayurvedic medicine to heal many skin disorders, from eczema and psoriasis to rashes and acne. You can add sliced burdock root to salads or juice it.

CABBAGE / Known for healing digestive ailments, cabbage juice is regarded as particularly effective in the treatment of ulcers because it is high in vitamin U. It is also high in sulfur, contains more vitamin C than oranges, and, along with other members of the brassica clan, is believed to inhibit the occurrence of certain types of cancers. Cabbage can be juiced or eaten raw.

CACAO / An amazing beauty food, cacao has the highest concentration of antioxidants of any food in the world! It is rich in chromium, manganese, zinc, iron, copper, and magnesium, all of which are essential trace minerals. Look for raw cacao powder and cacao nibs.

If you can't find cacao, you can snack on a small amount of dark chocolate.

CARROT / Carrot juice is full of beta-carotene, which is beneficial for your eyes and immune system. In traditional Chinese medicine, carrot juice is used for detoxifying the body and benefiting the eyes. Carrot is good for treating indigestion, overeating, and inflammation.

CELERY / This medicinal powerhouse contains essential oils that calm the nervous system and are effective in easing insomnia. Celery juice may also help lower blood pressure and reduce acidity in the body, and the presence of polyacetylene has been shown to lower inflammation. Celery also calms the liver and has a detoxifying effect.

CHIA SEEDS / Chia seeds are thought to help reduce inflammation, ease depression, and improve skin and hair health. Eating chia seeds gives us sustained energy and eating chia gel helps with hydration. Chia seeds are also a good source of omega-3s.

COCONUT / When the war against saturated fats began, coconut got a bad rap. But this powerful ingredient has made a major comeback. Populations that eat high concentrations of coconut have been shown to be some of the healthiest on earth, showing little evidence of heart disease. Coconut oil has a unique combination of fatty acids that have been shown to fight viruses, funguses, and harmful bacteria. Coconut is considered a good brain food, supplying energy for brain cells. It also decreases appetite and helps burn fat.

CUCUMBER / Cucumber juice contains soluble fiber, which assists nutrient absorption through the intestinal tract. Even though cucumbers are 96 percent water, their juice is rich in electrolytes that hydrate the body. Cool and sweet, cucumber is a natural diuretic. Cucumber juice is also rich in alkaline-forming minerals and is an excellent source of vitamins C and A, folate, manganese, molybdenum, potassium, silica, sulfur, and small amounts of vitamin B complex, sodium, calcium, phosphorus, and chlorine. The silica and sulfur support hair growth and healthy skin.

DANDELION / Known as *pu gong ying* in traditional Chinese medicine, dandelion greens are used to clear heat and toxins from the liver and stomach. We all know how it feels when we have had one too many glasses of wine and wake up feeling hot and thirsty at three o'clock in the morning. This is because alcohol is hot by nature and heats up the liver, and the liver has to filter the toxins of the alcohol. Drinking fresh dandelion juice will clear the heat and the toxins. Because the liver has so many jobs to do in the body, it is important to keep it healthy and happy at all times.

E3LIVE® / E3Live is a trademarked brand of an organic aqua-botanical algae. Packed with over 60 vitamins, minerals, and amino acids, it supports the immune, endocrine, nervous, gastrointestinal, and cardiovascular systems. It's also an incredible source of chlorophyll. With this abundance of natural nutrients, it's one of the most powerful and beneficial foods on the planet.

FENNEL / Fresh fennel juice is tops when it comes to vegetables that support digestion. Bloating, gas, intestinal cramps, and irritable bowels are all good reasons to drink fennel-rich Tummy Lover juice (PAGE 93). Fresh fennel juice is also chock-full of vitamin C, which is great for the immune system.

FLAXSEED / The flax plant produces seeds that are used both whole and ground and are also pressed for oil. The seeds and oil are rich in lignans, which contain plant estrogens that support healthy hormone balance and help reduce hot flashes. Flaxseeds also contain soluble and insoluble fiber, which can aid in easing constipation, and is full of omega-3 fatty acids, which help lower inflammation. Flaxseeds should be ground before eating.

FLAX OIL / Flax oil contains EFAs, which help to keep our cell membranes perm and healthy so they are able to let in nutritents, while keeping out toxins. Flax oil is yin in nature and is great for lubricating the skin and body. It works well for treating dry skin and hair. Flax oil is also rich in omega-3 fatty acids and substance called ALA, which has been shown to reduce inflammation and support a healthy heart. Please note that you should never heat flaxs oil, as it oxidizes quickly and loses potency.

GINGER / Ginger lowers inflammation, supports digestion, and reduces bloating and nausea. Warming in nature and a powerful antioxidant, it is used in traditional Chinese medicine for stomach ailments, to promote circulation, and to cure colds.

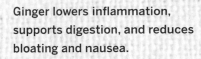

Ginger lowers inflammation, supports digestion, and reduces bloating and nausea.

This warming rhizome promotes circulation, treats cold symptoms, and soothes an upset stomach.

GINGER 姜

Kale is rich in many
vitamins, minerals,
chorophyll, and
antioxidants.

KALE

This bitter green
soothes congestion
and improves
stomach function.

GOJI BERRIES / Relatively new to the mainstream market, these superfoods, known as *gou qi zi,* have been used in Chinese medicine for thousands of years. They are used for eye health and clear vision, because they support the liver (the condition of the liver is reflected in the eyes). Goji berries also fortify the blood, so they are good for treating anemia. In addition, goji berries support the kidneys, so they can be helpful for tinnitus, since, according to Chinese medicine, the kidneys and the ears are connected by the same energy meridian.

GRAPEFRUIT / Cooling and sweet, grapefruit supports digestion and is rich in vitamin C, which helps to ward off colds. It has also been shown to lower cholesterol.

KALE / One of the most healthful members of the vegetable kingdom, kale is rich in vitamins A, K, and C; minerals like iron and calcium; and chlorophyll and antioxidants. Part of the mustard family, kale has compounds that have been shown to have anti-cancer properties. Kale also supports eye health and bone growth, and lowers inflammation. It is naturally warming and bitter and is used to soothe congestion and improve stomach function in traditional Chinese medicine.

LEMON / Outside of the body, lemon juice is an acid. But once you drink it, it has an alkaline effect—and a slightly alkaline body is what you want for optimal health. Cooling in nature, lemons aid digestion and have a cleansing effect. Lemons are also full of vitamin C, which is great for the immune system and boosts energy.

MINT / Fresh mint, which is pungent, aromatic, and cooling, promotes digestion and leaves you with a sweet fresh breath. In traditional Chinese medicine, this fragrant herb is used to brighten eyes, soothe a headache, support the liver, and clear up rashes.

MISO / A fermented probiotic food, miso helps to build good bacteria in the gut, so it strengthens the immune system. It contains the same kind of microorganisms that live in your large intestine, and as it ferments, those organisms grow, creating a healthy flora that does your body good. Try to find a soy-free miso that is made from brown rice, barley, chickpeas, or millet and that has been aged for a minimum of three years. I tend to skip soy-based miso because soy is hard to digest and creates a lot of phlegm in the body. My favorite miso products come from South River Miso Company.

ORANGE / Cooling, sweet, and rich in vitamin C, oranges are great for anyone who has dry eyes, skin, or nails. They are also good for combating dry mouth and hot flashes.

PARSLEY / Rich in energy-producing chlorophyll, parsley helps to build red blood cells, which translates to higher energy levels. It also freshens the breath and increases oxygenation of cells, supporting detoxification.

SPINACH / A nutritional power player, this dark leafy green helps to protect against many inflammatory issues, oxidative stress, and cardiovascular issues. Cool and sweet, spinach moistens dryness in the system. It is high in iron, and because a lack of iron equals a lack in energy, it is a good idea to add a few extra handfuls of spinach whenever you can!

STEVIA / A natural, safe, and calorie-free sweetener, stevia leaf extract is the ideal way to sweeten recipes lightly. Whole stevia leaves contain such nutrients as calcium, potassium, iron, phosphorus, magnesium, zinc, and niacin, many of which are known to help regulate blood sugar. Stevia might also help to lower blood pressure by preventing calcium from entering the blood stream, and it is believed to contain anti-inflammatory properties. It is a good sweetener choice for anyone trying to lose weight or modulate sugar intake. Although it has no glycemic impact or carbohydrates, it satisfies sweet cravings, and because of its primary sweetness compound, stevioside, it tastes up to 300 times sweeter than sugar. Stevia is available in both powder and liquid form. The latter, which is water extracted without the aid of chemicals and is thus less processed than the powder form, is recommended.

TOMATO / Excellent detoxifiers, tomatoes are alkalizing and purify the blood. Tomato juice is a great cure for a full stomach due to overeating and also clears liver heat, which makes it a successful treatment for migraines, hangovers, and dehydration. Cold, sweet, and sour, tomatoes strengthen the stomach and promote healthy digestion.

TURMERIC / Queen of all medicinal plants, fresh turmeric root and its antioxidative ingredient, curcumin, is thought to help reduce inflammation in the body, strengthen the immune system, and support overall health and wellness. It is used in traditional Chinese medicine to heal wounds, strengthen digestion, support liver health and detoxification, and lower inflammation, and is an important sattvic herb in ayurvedic medicine for its purifying and balancing properties. Turmeric strengthens the stomach and promotes healthy digestion, thanks to its cold, sweet, and sour properties.

TOMATO

番茄

Tomatoes are excellent
detoxifiers with alkalyzing
and purifying properties.

In TCM, tomatoes are
prescribed to clear
liver heat, which helps
treat migraines.

Specific Ailments and Foods That Treat Them

One of the best things about studying TCM was learning how common foods can treat everyday ailments. In this section, I'll share the edible remedies for typical complaints I hear from my patients. Please note that besides adding beneficial, healing foods, you'll want to cut the food items that may be exacerbating a given condition. I've included both the foods to add and the ones to avoid in this section.

ACNE, ROSACEA, AND FLARED SKIN

TRY Burdock root is a natural blood purifier. I have used the tincture in my practice with amazing results, especially with cystic acne.

AVOID Spicy foods and alcohol

WHY Burdock root purifies the blood and clears the skin from the inside out.

RECOMMENDED RECIPE Skin Beautiful juice (PAGE 133)

ALLERGIES (SEASONAL)

TRY In my practice, I have used the bioflavonoid quercetin (along with bromelain and nettles) with great success. I also use vitamin C as a natural antihistamine. I recommend taking 1,000 milligrams of vitamin C three to five times a day. Among the foods rich in quercetin are ancho chiles, buckwheat, capers, red grapes, blueberries, raspberries, red apples, cherries, blackberries, teas like rooibos and oat straw, and vegetables like onions, broccoli, and leafy greens. I suggest taking quercetin tablets, about 1 gram per day, for a couple of weeks to get the antiallergen substances into your system and then switching to food-based sources.

AVOID White sugar, white flour, alcohol, dairy products

WHY Quercetin has both antihistamine and anti-inflammatory properties.

RECOMMENDED RECIPE Vital Citrus Juice (PAGE 83)

BACK PAIN

TRY Turmeric root juice or powder

AVOID Inflammatory foods like white flour, white sugar, and processed foods

WHY Turmeric has long been used in both ayurvedic and Chinese medicine as an anti-inflammatory for pain and sore muscles.

RECOMMENDED RECIPE Turmeric Ginger Lemonade (PAGE 68)

BAD BREATH

TRY Parsley and chlorophyll

AVOID Spicy foods and dairy

WHY Parsley freshens breath and increases oxygenation of cells, which supports detoxification.

RECOMMENDED RECIPE Sweet Breath Juice (PAGE 138)

BLOATING AND WATER RETENTION

TRY Cucumber juice, watermelon juice, kombu kelp, lettuce, zucchini, pineapple, asparagus

AVOID Salt and foods that contain preservatives and flavor enhancers, such as monosodium glutamate, table salt, nitrates, and sulfites

WHY These foods are natural diuretics. Fluids move fluids, so drink lots of water and juices and eat foods that have a high water content.

RECOMMENDED RECIPE Cucumber Flush juice (PAGE 138)

THE ENERGETIC PROPERTIES OF FOOD IN TRADITIONAL CHINESE MEDICINE

Cold	Cool	Neutral	Warm/Hot
VEGETABLES			
Chinese cabbage, mung bean sprouts, sea vegetables, snow peas white mushrooms	alfalfa sprouts, artichokes, asparagus, beets, bok choy, broccoli, button mushrooms, cabbage, carrots, cauliflower, celery, corn, cucumber, dandelion greens, eggplant, potatoes, romaine lettuce, spinach, watercress, winter squash, zucchini	lettuce, Swiss chard, shiitake mushrooms, sweet potatoes	WARM bell pepper, green beans, kale, leeks, mustard greens, onions, parsley, parsnips HOT garlic, green onions
FRUITS			
Asian pears, bananas, cantaloupe, grapefruit, pears, watermelon	apples, apricots, figs, lemon, oranges, peaches, strawberries, tomatoes	mangoes, olives	cherries, coconut, grapes, pineapple, plums, raspberries, tangerines
GRAINS			
	millet, pearl barley, white rice, wheat	buckwheat, brown rice, cornmeal, rye	oats, sweet rice, wheat bran, wheat germ
BEANS, NUTS, AND SEEDS			
	mung beans, pumpkin seeds, soybeans, tofu	almonds, black sesame, hazelnuts, kidney beans, peanuts, peas, sunflower seeds	black beans, brown chestnuts, sesame seeds, lentils, pine nuts, walnuts
ANIMAL PRODUCTS			
pork	chicken eggs, clams, crab	ocean fish, gelatin, dairy, oysters	WARM beef, chicken, freshwater fish, shrimp, turkey HOT lamb
HERBS			
cassia seeds, chrysanthemum, honeysuckle flower	cilantro, mint	licorice root	WARM anise, basil, cardamom, clove, coriander seed, fennel seed, fresh ginger HOT black pepper, cinnamon, dried ginger
MISCELLANEOUS			
salt, vitamin C, white sugar	green tea	honey, barley malt	brown sugar, coffee, molasses, rice vinegar, wine

CRAMPS + PMS

Avocado

Spinach

Cacao

Almonds

Lentils

CONSTIPATION

TRY Eat foods that moisten the intestines and promote bowel movements, such as prunes, pears, apples, bananas, flaxseeds, papayas, cascara root, wheatgrass, spirulina, and green juices, as well as probiotics and foods that promote beneficial flora, like miso, coconut kefir, and fermented beverages. Drink at least 8 glasses of water daily and plenty of fresh vegetable juice.

AVOID Processed foods and meat that can clog the system and foods devoid of fiber and nutrients, which tend to block the energy in the GI tract

WHY It helps clean your system and gets the bowels moving.

RECOMMENDED RECIPE Ensalada Verde (PAGE 75)

CRAMPS AND PMS

TRY Eat food rich in magnesium, such as spinach, lentils, pumpkin seeds, almonds, avocados, and cacao.

AVOID Sugar and alcohol

WHY Minerals like magnesium and wpotassium help stimulate activity in your muscles and nerves.

RECOMMENDED RECIPE PMS Relief (PAGE 138)

FATIGUE AND INSOMNIA

TRY Celery juice. About an hour before bedtime, drink a large glass that contains a good amount of celery juice. Combined with an acupuncture session, this is amazing for calming the nervous system and supporting a great night's sleep. Try, also, not eating for 2–3 hours before bedtime.

AVOID Rich foods, spicy foods, coffee and caffeine in other forms, and alcohol.

WHY Celery helps to regulate the nervous system and promotes a sense of well-being.

RECOMMENDED RECIPE Sweet Greens Sleep Juice (PAGE 134)

HANGOVER

TRY Green juice that contains dandelion greens, turmeric, and beets. Or, try wheatgrass, spirulina, carrot juice, and fennel juice. Drink lots of water.

AVOID Alcohol, fried foods, sugar

WHY Green juice and dandelion greens help to cool and cleanse the liver after a night of partying. Beets cleanse the liver and purify the blood, and turmeric is an anti-inflammatory and benefits the liver. Greens like wheatgrass and spirulina cool the liver, and carrot juice supports the function of the liver. Fennel helps with digestion, which can help some people when they have a hangover.

RECOMMENDED RECIPE Dandelion Liver Tonic (PAGE 82)

HEARTBURN

TRY Cabbage juice is the best choice. Other foods that help with heartburn are apples, ginger, papayas, pineapple, and carrots.

AVOID Hot and spicy foods, fried foods, and foods that contain white flour and white sugar

WHY Cabbage juice contains vitamin U (which, despite the name, is actually an enzyme) that some believe helps heal GI tract ailments and reduces pain and inflammation. Drink it two to three times daily. You can mix it with other juices so it tastes better.

RECOMMENDED RECIPE Tummy Lover Juice (PAGE 93)

HIGH BLOOD PRESSURE

TRY Beet juice, ginger, and turmeric

AVOID Salt, alcohol, and fatty foods

WHY Beet juice lowers blood pressure and ginger and turmeric reduce inflammation. Ginger helps to lower high blood pressure by the same action that promotes circulation in the body. The anti-inflammatory properties of turmeric support cardiovascular function, which helps lower blood pressure.

RECOMMENDED RECIPE Beetnik (PAGE 130)

HOT FLASHES

TRY Foods that tonify the yin, especially flaxseeds and primrose oil, plus bananas, nori, quinoa, spirulina, beets, raspberries, eggs, and Alkalizing Mineral Broth (PAGE 64). Add flaxseed meal or primrose oil to a morning smoothie. Eat lots of leafy greens, drink plenty of water, and make green juices without added fruit. Along with diet, acupuncture and herbal therapy are effective at diminishing hot flashes and balancing the body during menopause.

AVOID Spicy foods, caffeine, and alcohol

WHY Yin is the fluids that cool the body, so when you're deficient in yin, you have too much heat (yang). You must avoid spicy foods, as they increase the yang in your body, which prevents you from cooling down.

RECOMMENDED RECIPE Antioxidant Green Smoothie (PAGE 75) with 1 tablespoon flax oil.

INSOMNIA. SEE FATIGUE

METABOLIC SYNDROME

TRY Foods rich in chromium (found in broccoli, barley, and green beans), cinnamon, green tea, flaxseeds, and soaked nuts and seeds. Eat fresh vegetables, low-glycemic fruits like apples, berries, and grapefruit, and use sweeteners like stevia or xylitol instead of sugar. Incorporate healthy fats into your diet, especially avocado, coconut oil, and raw nuts and seeds.

AVOID Processed foods, fruit juices, sodas, and any foods that contain white sugar and other sweeteners

WHY Metabolic syndrome (aka syndrome X), a prediabetic condition, is primarily a result of the high consumption of sugars and high-glycemic foods. Foods containing chromium, cinnamon, green tea, flaxseeds, and soaked nuts and seeds all support healthy blood sugar levels. Foods rich in healthy fats slow the breakdown of sugar in the body for sustained energy and contribute to balanced blood sugar levels. Combining exercise with a low-glycemic diet works wonders to combat this syndrome.

RECOMMENDED RECIPE Blueberry-Goji-Açai Smoothie (PAGE 145) with ½ teaspoon ground cinnamon stirred in.

MIGRAINE AND CHRONIC HEADACHE

TRY Green juice made with dandelion greens. Adopting a healthy diet that includes lots of leafy greens is a good idea. In TCM, migraines are related to imbalances in the liver. Acupuncture therapy is a good addition to a healthy diet.

AVOID Hot and spicy foods, coffee and caffeine in other forms, and alcohol. Some people suffering from migraines have identified a trigger food; once you have determined a trigger food, be sure to remove it from your diet. Stress is also

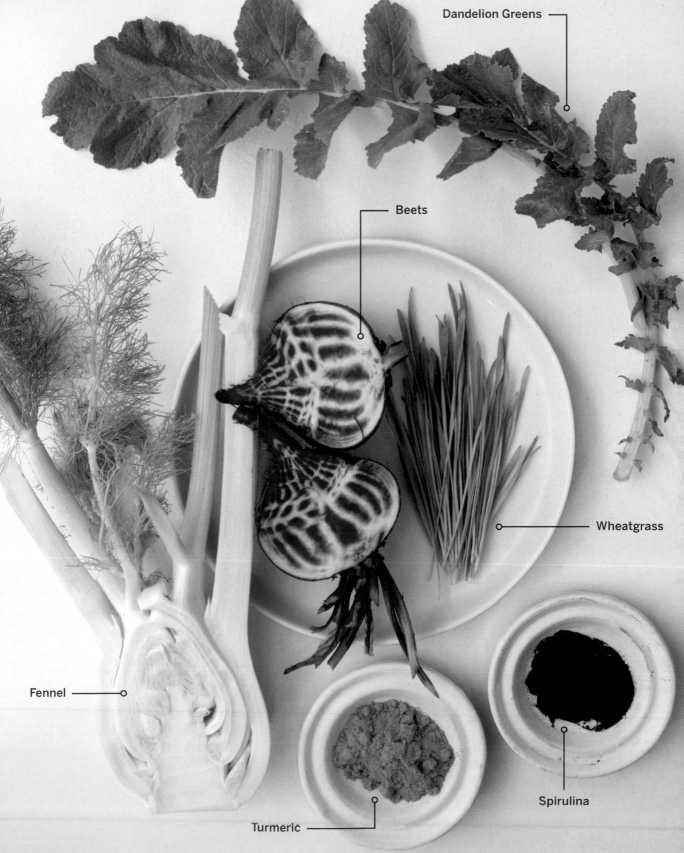

AILMENT
HANGOVER

Dandelion Greens

Beets

Wheatgrass

Fennel

Turmeric

Spirulina

one of the major factors in liver imbalances, so removing stress from your life is critical for treating headaches.

WHY Green juice helps to cool and calm the liver, an organ that, according to traditional Chinese medicine, is almost always involved in the occurrence of migraine headaches.

RECOMMENDED RECIPE Headache Relief (PAGE 137)

NAUSEA

TRY Juices or foods made with ginger or mint. Also, try crushing a tablespoon of fennel seeds, put them in a teacup, add hot water, and let steep for a few minutes before sipping.

AVOID Greasy foods

WHY Ginger and mint are natural antinausea foods. Ginger also helps to reduce gas and bloating. Fennel seeds, or *xiao hui xiang*, harmonize the stomach. Cardamom, or *sha ren*, can transform phlegm and calm the stomach.

RECOMMENDED RECIPE Pink Juice for the Tummy (PAGE 138) or Cashew-Cardamom Milk (PAGE 141).

PMS. SEE CRAMPS

PRE-DIABETES / TYPE 2 DIABETES

TRY Fresh vegetables and low-glycemic fruits (apples, berries, grapefuit); healthy fats; high-quality protein

AVOID White potatoes, sugar, white flour–based products, soda, candy, chips and crackers, and alcohol

WHY Eating a diet high in sugar and simple carbs can, over time, create high blood sugar

levels that can lead to pre-diabetes and type 2 diabetes. This type of diet also leads to higher levels of inflammation in the body. In addition to the foods recommended above, choose healthy fats like coconut oil and cold-pressed flax and olive oils; quality proteins like hemp seeds, spirulina, almonds, cashews, and chia seeds. If you eat animal protein, try to choose organic and pastured meats, eggs, and cheeses that are made without the use of antibiotics or hormones. Drink lots of green juice and choose stevia as your sweetener.

RECOMMENDED RECIPES Raspberry Superfood Smoothie (PAGE 146)

RED, IRRITATED EYES

TRY Goji berries and mint tea

AVOID Alcohol, spicy foods, fried foods, and harsh makeup

WHY Goji berries, known in Chinese as *gou qi zi*, are used in traditional Chinese medicine to brighten and nourish the eyes. Mint, known as *bo he*, helps to clear heat from burning red eyes.

RECOMMENDED RECIPE Tea for Clear Eyes (PAGE 138)

URINARY TRACT INFECTION (UTI)

TRY Cranberries, carrot, celery, asparagus, lemons, and dandelion greens. If you try cranberry juice, be sure to purchase unsweetened juice and sweeten it with stevia, as juice sweetened with sugar may aggravate the condition. Drink lots of water. Try adding D-Mannose (a powder that can be found in vitamin stores or health food stores, which can be a game changer for chronic UTI sufferers. D-Mannose is a simple sugar that binds to e-coli bacteria, which are the cause of the majority of UTIs. I've found that for some people, D-Mannose is more effective than antibiotics.

AVOID Sugar, processed or greasy foods, alcohol, coffee, and foods high in carbohydrates

WHY Cranberry soothes the urinary tract and supports its healthy functioning. In Chinese medicine, too much heat in the bladder meridian is believed to be the cause of urinary tract infections, and cranberry is thought to clear the troubling heat and toxins. Celery and asparagus help clear heat by promoting urination. Carrot supports the immune system. According to TCM, dandelion clears damp heat toxins, which is equivalent to clearing infection.

RECOMMENDED RECIPE Cool Down Juice (PAGE 137)

YEAST INFECTION

TRY Probiotics and cultured foods, as well as foods that have antifungal properties, like coconut and its oil. Eat lots of non-starchy vegetables.

AVOID Sugar and all foods that contain sugar, including fruit, and complex carbohydrates. Also avoid alcohol, mushrooms, aged cheeses, vinegar (apple cider vinegar is okay), and foods that contain gluten.

WHY Yeast thrives on sugar, which is why sugar must be avoided. Probiotics and cultured foods, such as raw sauerkraut and kefir, will help fight off the yeast bacteria that is causing the infection.

RECOMMENDED RECIPE Fermented Salad (PAGE 150)

RECIPES

As much as I create recipes for their nutritional value and cleansing properties, I always strive to design dishes that taste great. I live for flavor and I never compromise my enjoyment when thinking through a healthy recipe. Most all of these recipes are low-glycemic, supporting vital health, and these dishes are proof positive that healthy food can taste amazing. In fact, I'm so confident in the taste of these dishes that I serve them to guests—and often receive enthusiastic compliments. One friend who just did the cleanse reports that the Asian Kale Salad (PAGE 77) is the best salad she's ever eaten—in her life. I'm thrilled to be able to share these creations with you, because I know they'll help you heal—and make you happy. Whether you continue your cleanse or just want to add healthy meals to your repertoire, you're going to thoroughly enjoy these selections.

BREAKFAST

These breakfast dishes are my four personal favorites. Besides providing a good dose of nutrients for energy during the day, they are delicious and satisfying. And don't forget the breakfast recipes I included in the cleanse section, like the raw granola and the meal-like smoothies. With all these types of breakfast items from savory to sweet, you'll always find something filling, flavorful, and full of nutrients to start your day.

CHIA PUDDING PARFAIT

This morning parfait is not only beautiful to look at but also tastes like heaven on earth. The chia base is rich in essential fatty acids and supports energy levels, making this a great way to start the day.

> 1 cup (8 fl oz/250 ml) Chia Gel (page 75)
> ⅓ cup (3 fl oz/80 ml) Cashew Milk (page 141)
> Pinch of Himalayan pink salt
> ¼ teaspoon alcohol-free vanilla extract
> 4 drops liquid stevia
> ¼ cup (1 oz/30 g) fresh raspberries
> ¼ cup (1 oz/30 g) blueberries, plus a few for garnish
> ¼ cup (1¼ oz/35 g) chopped banana

In a bowl, combine the chia gel and cashew milk. Stir well. Add the salt, vanilla, and stevia and stir until blended. Put the raspberries in the bottom of a parfait glass. Spoon one-half of the chia–cashew milk mixture over the raspberries. Top with the blueberries, followed by the banana. Top with the remaining chia–cashew milk mixture and garnish with blueberries. Serve right away.

Makes 1 serving

STEAMED GREENS WITH POACHED EGGS

Eggs boost blood and the yin in your body, are high in vitamins A and B, and are a good source of protein. The yolk, rather than the white, holds this rich array of nutrients. Whenever possible, use organic omega-3 rich eggs from pastured hens.

> 1 bunch rainbow chard
> ½ bunch lacinato kale
> Filtered water
> 1½ teaspoons coconut oil
> Sea salt and freshly ground black pepper
> ½ cup (4 fl oz/125 ml) apple cider vinegar
> 2 organic eggs from pastured hens

Remove the stems from the chard and kale and tear the leaves into small pieces. Pour filtered water to a depth of 2 inches (5 cm) into the base of a steamer and bring to a boil. Arrange the greens on the steamer rack, cover, and steam until lightly wilted, 1–2 minutes.

Transfer the greens to a bowl, drizzle with the coconut oil, sprinkle with ½ teaspoon salt, and toss to coat evenly. Transfer to a plate and set aside.

To poach the eggs, divide the vinegar evenly between 2 small bowls. Crack 1 egg into each bowl, taking care not to break the yolk. Let the eggs stand for 5 minutes.

Meanwhile, pour filtered water to a depth of about 3 inches (7.5 cm) into a saucepan and bring the water to a boil over high heat. After the eggs have stood for 5 minutes, using a whisk, swirl the boiling water to create a whirlpool effect, then carefully slip 1 egg with its vinegar into center of the whirlpool. Continue to swirl the water around the perimeter of the pan until the water returns to a boil. The egg white will begin to wrap around the yolk. As soon as the water returns to a boil, reduce the heat to medium and gently simmer the egg, frequently swirling the water, until the white is just set and the yolk is still runny, about 2 minutes. Using a slotted spoon, gently remove the egg from the water and place it on paper towels to gently blot it dry. Repeat with the remaining egg.

Season the eggs with salt and pepper, then carefully place them atop the wilted greens to serve.

Makes 1 serving

Chia Pudding Parfait, opposite page

Acai Bowl, opposite page

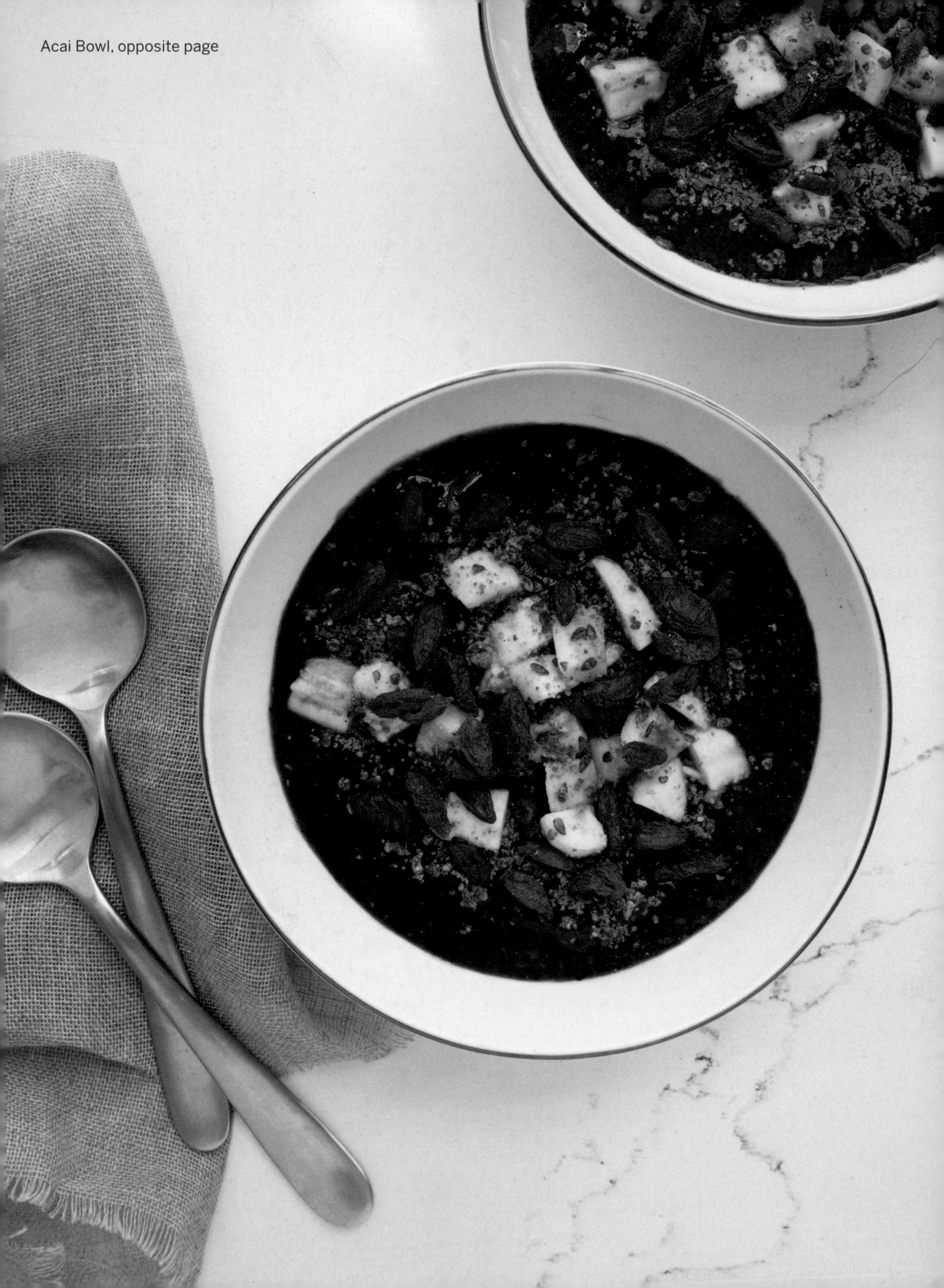

POACHED EGGS WITH AVOCADO SALSA AND CILANTRO

This simple breakfast dish is loaded with health benefits. Avocado is good for the skin and builds blood and yin. It is also rich in lecithin, which makes it a brain food! Tomato is a detoxifier and supports liver cleansing. Because it clears liver heat, it is great for treating a hangover or detoxing from medications. Cilantro helps draw heavy metals out of the body.

1 avocado, halved, pitted, peeled, and cut into 1-inch (2.5-inch) chunks

1 cup (6 oz/185 g) cherry tomatoes, halved

Leaves from 1 bunch fresh cilantro, coarsely chopped

Juice of 3 limes

¼ jalapeño chile, finely chopped

1 teaspoon sea salt

½ cup (4 fl oz/125 ml) apple cider vinegar

Filtered water

2 organic eggs from pastured hens

In a bowl, combine the avocado, tomatoes, and cilantro. Drizzle with the lime juice, sprinkle with the chile and salt, and toss to mix evenly. Set aside.

To poach the eggs, divide the vinegar evenly between 2 small bowls. Crack 1 egg into each bowl, taking care not to break the yolk. Let the eggs stand for 5 minutes.

Meanwhile, pour filtered water to a depth of about 3 inches (7.5 cm) into a saucepan and bring the water to a boil over high heat. When the eggs have stood for 5 minutes, using a whisk, swirl the boiling water to create a whirlpool effect, then carefully slip 1 egg with its vinegar into center of the whirlpool. Continue to swirl the water around the perimeter of the pan until the water returns to a boil. The egg white will begin to wrap around the yolk. As soon as the water returns to a boil, reduce the heat to medium and gently simmer the egg, frequently swirling the water, until the white is just set and the yolk is still runny, about 2 minutes. Using a slotted spoon, gently remove the egg from the water and place it on paper towels to gently blot it dry. Repeat with the remaining egg.

Carefully transfer the eggs to a plate and smother them with the salsa mixture. Serve right away.

Makes 1 serving

AÇAI BOWL

Every ingredient in this recipe is great for you. Açai, blueberries, and raspberries contain large amounts of antioxidants and are low-glycemic foods. Chia gel carries essential fatty acids for healthy skin and hair, as well as energy. And spirulina contains one of the most bioavailable proteins on the planet. The açai berry, which has been a dietary staple of the Amazon basin tribes for centuries, has only recently been recognized for its wealth of antioxidants, which help to quell the free radicals that are responsible for aging, disease, and oxidation.

1 bag (3½ oz/105 g) frozen açai berries

½ cup (2½ oz/75 g) frozen blueberries

½ cup (4 oz/125 g) frozen raspberries

½ cup (4 fl oz/125 ml) Chia Gel (page 75)

1 tablespoon spirulina powder

1 banana, peeled and halved

10 raw almonds

2 tablespoons flaxseeds

⅛ teaspoon sea salt

¼ teaspoon ground cinnamon

¼ teaspoon alcohol-free vanilla extract

In a food processor, combine the açai berries, blueberries, raspberries, Chia Gel, spirulina, and half of the banana and process until smooth. Transfer to a bowl and set aside. Rinse out and dry the food processor.

In the food processor, combine the almonds, flaxseeds, salt, cinnamon, and vanilla and pulse until the mixture is the consistency of fine meal.

Chop the remaining banana half and scatter it over the berry mixture. Top with the flaxseed-almond mixture and serve right away.

Makes 1 serving

JUICES

Fresh juices rapidly supply the body with health-promoting enzymes, vitamins, minerals, pigments, and phytonutrients. The workforce of the body, enzymes are essential for digesting food and producing energy and are critical for most of the body's metabolic activities. Consuming juices also floods your cells with the healing benefits of the fruits and vegetables from which they are made, cleanses the body on a cellular level, and contributes to a healthy alkaline balance. Regularly consuming plenty of fresh vegetable and fruit juices offers many benefits:

○ Boosts immune system

○ Increases energy

○ Improves endocrine functions

○ Provides rest for the digestive organs

○ Encourages physical rejuvenation

○ Promotes healthy body weight

○ Promotes normalized blood pressure

○ Reverses signs of aging

○ Promotes mental well-being

○ Alleviates symptoms of pms

○ Promotes clear skin

○ Improves allergies

○ Supports fertility

In addition to what you see here, look for other juices in the 4-day cleanse on pages 58–94. Use well-washed organic ingredients for your juices whenever possible.

PINK LEMONADE

Beets give this lemonade its beautiful color. The addition of ginger delivers a pleasant zesty flavor. Sweet and cool, beets support detoxification, build the blood, and help with constipation. Apple juice is cooling and contains soluble fiber. Fresh ginger supports digestion.

½ beet

2 Fuji apples

2 small lemons, peeled

1-inch (2.5-cm) knob fresh ginger

1½ cups (12 fl oz/375 ml) filtered water

Cut the beet and apples as needed into pieces that will fit into the chute of your extraction juicer. Then, following the manufacturer's instructions, juice the beet, apples, lemons, and ginger in that order. Add the water, stir to mix, and pour into a tall glass.

Makes 1 serving

BEETNIK

A nutritional powerhouse, beets support a healthy bloody pressure. If you suffer from chronically high blood pressure, however, you should consult a physician. Carrots support digestion and are rich in beta-carotene, which contributes to a healthy immune system.

1–2 beets

1 Granny Smith apple

1-inch (2.5-cm) knob fresh turmeric

1-inch (2.5-cm) knob ginger

5–6 carrots

Cut the vegetables and the apple as needed into pieces that will fit into the chute of your extraction juicer. Then, following the manufacturer's instructions, juice all of the ingredients in the order given. Pour into a tall glass.

Makes 1 serving

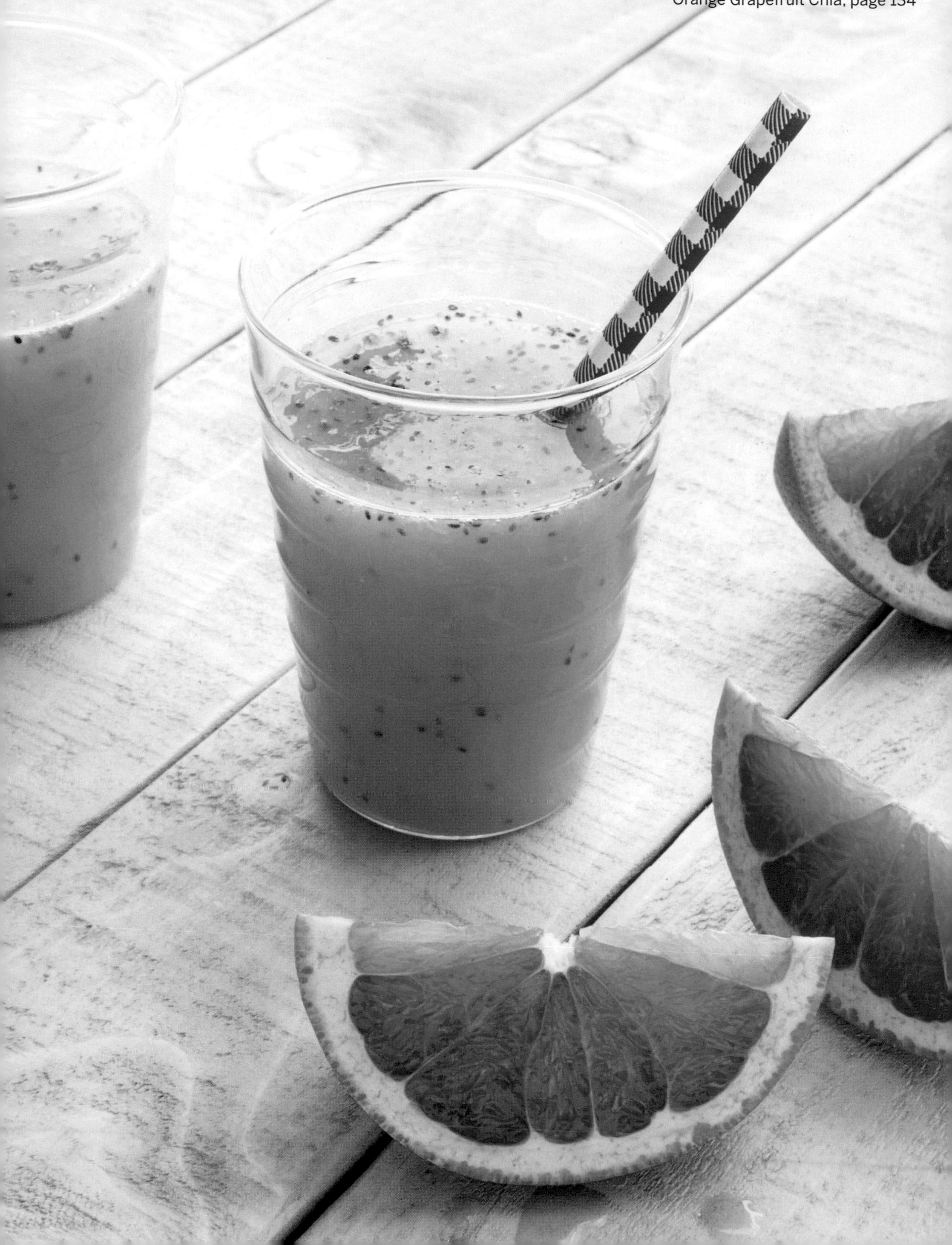

Orange Grapefruit Chia, page 134

Skin Beautiful, opposite page

BURDOCK SKIN CLEANSE

Make this juice when you want to clear up acne, a rash, or other skin imbalance. Scrub the burdock root well to dislodge any clinging dirt. The beta-carotene in carrots supports healthy and glowing skin. Parsley is cooling and helps clear the eyes.

- 1 cucumber
- 4 celery ribs
- ¼ bunch fresh flat-leaf parsley
- 1–2 cups (1–2 oz/30–60 g) spinach leaves
- 2 kale leaves
- ¼ burdock root
- 3 carrots

Cut the vegetables as needed into pieces that will fit into the chute of your extraction juicer. Then, following the manufacturer's instructions, juice all of the ingredients in the order given. Pour into a tall glass.

Makes 1 serving

SKIN BEAUTIFUL

Cucumbers are rich in silica, which promotes glowing skin and hair. Dandelion greens support liver health, which is an important factor for beautiful skin. Be sure to wash the burdock root well, as dirt can cling to its rough brown skin.

- 4 celery ribs
- ¼ bunch fresh flat-leaf parsley
- 1–2 cups (1–2 oz/30–60 g) spinach leaves
- 2 kale leaves
- ½ burdock root
- ¼ bunch dandelion greens
- 1 green apple
- 1¼ cucumbers

Cut the vegetables and the apple as needed into pieces that will fit into the chute of your extraction juicer. Then, following the manufacturer's instructions, juice all of the ingredients in the order given. Pour into a tall glass.

Makes 1 serving

WATERMELON, CUCUMBER, AND KALE JUICE

Don't worry about removing the seeds in this cooling juice. If your fruit is organic, you can juice part of the watermelon rind, which supports healthy skin and has other medicinal qualities. Replace up to one-fourth of the total weight of the fruit with the rind.

- 1 lb (500 g) watermelon
- 5 large kale leaves
- 1 cucumber

Cut the watermelon, kale, and cucumber as needed into pieces that will fit into the chute of your extraction juicer. Then, following the manufacturer's instructions, juice all of the ingredients in the order given. Pour into a tall glass.

Makes 1 serving

E3LIVE® ENERGY GREEN

This juice will make you glow from the inside out. E3Live, a brand of highly nutritious blue-green algae, is a great energy booster and promotes optimal health. This is my go-to juice most mornings. It gives me enough energy so that I don't need caffeine to get moving.

- 2 kale leaves
- ¼ bunch fresh flat-leaf parsley
- 1–2 cups (1–2 oz/30–60 g) spinach leaves
- 4 celery ribs
- 1 cucumber
- 1 tablespoon E3Live

Cut the vegetables as needed into pieces that will fit into the chute of your extraction juicer. Then, following the manufacturer's instructions, juice the kale, parsley, spinach, celery, and cucumber in the order given. Pour into a tall glass and stir in the E3Live.

Makes 1 serving

CHLOROPHYLL LEMONADE

This delicious, apple-flavored lemonade also great for freshening the breath. Chlorphyll is similar in structure to red blood cells, so it helps build the blood and increase energy and oxygenation of the cells.

- 3 cups (3 oz/90 g) spinach leaves
- 2 Fuji apples
- 2 lemons, peeled
- 1½ cups (12 fl oz/375 ml) filtered water
- Liquid stevia, for sweetening (optional)

Cut the apples and lemons as needed into pieces that will fit into the chute of your extraction juicer. Then, following the manufacturer's instructions, juice the spinach, apples, and lemons in that order. Add the water, stir to mix, and sweeten with stevia, if desired. Pour into a tall glass.
Makes 1 serving

ORANGE GRAPEFRUIT CHIA

Packed with vitamin C, energy-boosting chia seeds, and a big dose of omega-3 fatty acids, this tasty juice is guaranteed to get you out the door in the morning.

- 1 pink grapefruit, peeled
- 3 juice oranges, peeled
- 1 tablespoon chia seeds

Cut the fruits as needed into pieces that will fit into the chute of your extraction juicer. Then, following the manufacturer's instructions, juice the fruits. Pour into a tall glass, add the seeds, and stir well to prevent the seeds from sticking together.
Makes 1 serving

SPICY LEMONADE

Here is a low-glycemic, spicy juice that will get your metabolism going; it's a great drink to support weight loss. Cayenne pepper stimulates the metabolism and helps blood circulation.

- 2 lemons, peeled
- 2 cups (15 fl oz/500 ml) filtered water
- ¼ teaspoon cayenne pepper
- Liquid stevia, for sweetening

Cut the lemons if needed into pieces that will fit into the chute of your extraction juicer. Then, following the manufacturer's instructions, juice the lemons. Add the water, cayenne, and stevia to taste and stir well. Pour into a tall glass.
Makes 1 serving

SWEET GREENS SLEEP JUICE

The watercress and romaine lettuce used here are high in calcium, which helps the body to relax after a long day, and the citrus fruits are believed to enhance your REM sleep. Among its other health-promoting properties, celery contains essential oils that help calm the nervous system.

- 1 large orange, peeled
- ½ lemon, peeled
- ¼ bunch watercress
- ¼ head romaine lettuce
- 4 celery ribs

Cut the vegetables and fruits as needed into pieces that will fit into the chute of your extraction juicer. Then, following the manufacturer's instructions, juice all of the ingredients in the order given. Pour into a tall glass.
Makes 1 serving

BLOODY GREAT

A truly detoxifying juice, this flavorful concoction is great for a hangover—and even better without one! Tomatoes are excellent for detoxification. Cilantro has cleansing properties that pull heavy metals away from the body. Cucumber helps flush away toxins.

- ¼ cup (¼ oz/7 g) fresh cilantro leaves
- ½ fresh red chile, seeded
- 2–3 tomatoes
- 5 celery ribs
- 1 red bell pepper
- 3 limes, peeled
- ½ cucumber

Pink Lemonade, page 130

Tea for Clear Eyes,
page 138

Cut the vegetables as needed into pieces that will fit into the chute of your extraction juicer. Then, following the manufacturer's instructions, juice all of the ingredients in the order given. Pour into a tall glass.

Makes 1 serving

APPLE-WHEATGRASS BLAST

Sweetened with apple juice and spiced with ginger, this chlorophyll-rich wheatgrass juice is guaranteed to give you a glow. Wheatgrass is one of nature's best superfoods. Brimming with chlorophyll, it floods the cells with nutrients and helps increase energy. Ginger supports digestion and lowers inflammation.

- 2 Granny Smith apples
- 2 lemons, peeled
- 1-inch (2.5-cm) knob fresh ginger
- ¼ cup (2 fl oz/60 ml) thawed frozen liquid wheatgrass
- ½ cup (4 fl oz/125 ml) filtered water

Cut the apples and lemons as needed into pieces that will fit into the chute of your extraction juicer. Then, following the manufacturer's instructions, juice the apples, lemons, and ginger in that order. Add the wheatgrass and water and stir to mix well. Pour into a tall glass.

Makes 1 serving

BLOOD PURIFIER WITH BURDOCK AND DANDELION

This bitter, medicinal-tasting juice is great when you want that extra cleansing punch! Dandelion greens support liver detoxification and function. It's especially great to drink after finishing a course of medication or after drinking alcohol.

- ¼ bunch dandelion greens
- 4 celery ribs
- ¼ bunch fresh flat-leaf parsley,
- 1–2 cups (1–2 oz/30–60 g) spinach leaves
- 2 kale leaves
- ½ burdock root
- 1 cucumber

Cut the vegetables as needed into pieces that will fit into the chute of your extraction juicer. Then, following the manufacturer's instructions, juice all of the ingredients in the order given. Pour into a tall glass.

Makes 1 serving

COOL DOWN JUICE

This juice alkalinizes the body, reduces inflammation, and clears heat. This is a great juice to combat burning when urinating or a urinary tract infection. Its ingredients help to flush excess water from the body and clear heat.

- 4 carrots
- 5 celery ribs
- 4 dandelion leaves
- 1 lemon, peeled
- 2 asparagus spears
- 1 cucumber

Cut the vegetables and lemon as needed into pieces that will fit into the chute of your extraction juicer. Then, following the manufacturer's instructions, juice all of the ingredients in the order given. Pour into a tall glass.

Makes 1 serving

HEADACHE RELIEF

In TCM, headaches are related to imbalances in the liver. This juice contains ingredients that support the liver and cool heat.

- ¼ bunch dandelion greens
- 4 celery ribs
- 3 carrots
- 1–2 cups (1–2 oz/30–60 g) spinach leaves
- 2 kale leaves
- 1 apple
- 1 cucumber

Cut the vegetables and the apple as needed into pieces that will fit into the chute of your extraction juicer. Then, following the manufacturer's instructions, juice all of the ingredients in the order given. Pour into a tall glass.

Makes 1 serving

SWEET BREATH JUICE

This juice is rich in chlorophyll from the parsley, while the carrots in the recipe support good digestion.

½ bunch fresh flat-leaf parsley

2 carrots

1 cup (1 oz/30 g) spinach leaves

5 celery ribs

½ cucumber

Cut the vegetables as needed into pieces that will fit into the chute of your extraction juicer. Then, following the manufacturer's instructions, juice all of the ingredients in the order given. Pour into a tall glass.

Makes 1 serving

CUCUMBER FLUSH

This juice, which is a natural diuretic, is perfect for those days when you feel like you are holding a little extra water. It's also great for combating PMS and bloating.

1½ cucumbers

1 daikon radish

1 Granny Smith apple

1-inch (2.5-cm) knob fresh ginger

Cut the vegetables and apple as needed into pieces that will fit into the chute of your extraction juicer. Then, following the manufacturer's instructions, juice all of the ingredients in the order given. Pour into a tall glass.

Makes 1 serving

PMS RELIEF

Fennel is a uterine tonic, which makes it a soothing choice for any premenstrual symptoms.

½ fennel bulb

4 large mustard green leaves

½ bunch fresh flat-leaf parsley

5 carrots

1 Granny Smith apple

Cut the vegetables and the apple as needed into pieces that will fit into the chute of your extraction juicer. Then, following the manufacturer's instructions, juice all of the ingredients in the order given. Pour into a tall glass.

Makes 1 serving

PINK JUICE FOR THE TUMMY

This light, refreshing lemonade supports good digestion and helps treat nausea.

1-inch (2.5-cm) knob fresh ginger

¼ bunch fresh mint

1 slice beet, 1 inch (2.5 cm) thick

2 Fuji apples

¾–1 cup (6–8 fl oz/180–250 ml) filtered water

Cut the apples as needed into pieces that will fit into the chute of your extraction juicer. Then, following the manufacturer's instructions, juice the ginger, mint, beet, and apples in that order. Add the water, stir to mix, and pour into a tall glass.

Makes 1 serving

TEA FOR CLEAR EYES

This infusion is great for treating red, irritated eyes or puffiness. The mint is cooling, and in TCM it is used to brighten the eyes. Goji berries, or *gou qi zi*, contribute to eye health and nourish the yin.

2 cups (16 fl oz/500 ml) filtered water

¼ cup (1 oz/30 g) dried goji berries

Leaves from ½ bunch fresh peppermint or spearmint

Liquid stevia, for sweetening

In a small saucepan, bring the water to a boil over high heat. Immediately remove from the heat, add the goji berries and mint, and let steep for 10 minutes. Pour into a large mug, sweeten with stevia to taste, and enjoy.

Makes 1 serving

Bloody Great, page 134

Almond Milk, page 142

NUT MILKS

Sprouted cashews and almonds, the basis of two popular nut milks, are chock-full of essential minerals like manganese, potassium, copper, iron, magnesium, and zinc. They also contain selenium, a micronutrient that supports healthy detoxification. Cinnamon is added not only added for its delicious flavor but also for its ability to balance blood sugar levels and, according to Chinese medicine, to ward off colds, support the kidneys, warm the body, and get the circulation moving. Like cinnamon, vanilla contributes wonderful flavor, and is also rich in antioxidants. These creamy blends will also soothe and relax you.

CASHEW MILK

This is a simple, creamy treat on its own, but also can be used as a base for a variety of nut milk combinations and other nourishing recipes.

> 4 cups (32 fl oz/1 l) water
> 1 cup (5 oz/155 g) Soaked Cashews (page 168)
> 1 tablespoon alcohol-free vanilla extract
> ¼ teaspoon liquid stevia
> ½ teaspoon ground cinnamon

In a blender, combine all of the ingredients and blend on high speed for 45 seconds. Pour the mixture through a nut-milk bag or fine-mesh sieve. Pour into a tightly closed jar and store in the refrigerator for up to 3 days.
Makes about 5 cups (40 fl oz/1.25 l)

CARROT-CASHEW MILK

Rich in vitamin A, this drink includes the spiciness of ginger and the natural sweetness of carrot.

> 1½ cups (12 fl oz/375 ml) Cashew Milk (above)
> ½ cup (4 fl oz/125 ml) fresh carrot juice
> 1 tablespoon ginger juice (TIP: juice a ¼-inch/6-mm knob ginger along with the carrots)

In a blender, combine all of the ingredients and blend on high speed for 45 seconds. Pour the mixture through a nut-milk bag or fine-mesh sieve into a tall glass.
Makes 1 serving

WARM TURMERIC MILK

This is my take on a traditional Indian Ayurvedic hot drink. I use cashew milk instead of cow's milk along with fresh turmeric and ginger. It is soothing and great for boosting the immune system, helping address the symptoms of colds, flu, and sore throats.

> 2 cups (16 fl oz/500 ml) Cashew Milk (left)
> 1-inch (2.5-cm) knob turmeric, finely grated
> 1-inch (2.5-cm) knob ginger, finely grated
> Small pinch freshly ground black pepper
> 1 tablespoon local honey

In a small saucepan over medium heat, warm the cashew milk. While it is warming, add the turmeric, ginger, and pepper stirring well. Let cook on low heat until simmering, 2–3 minutes. Remove from the heat and let stand for 10–12 minutes. Strain the mixture into a mug and stir in the honey.
Makes 1 serving

CASHEW-CARDAMOM MILK

This spice-laced milk tastes amazing and will soothe an upset tummy.

> 2 cups (16 fl oz/500 ml) Cashew Milk (left)
> ⅛ teaspoon ground cinnamon
> ¼ teaspoon ground ginger
> ⅛ teaspoon ground cardamom
> Pinch freshly ground black pepper

In a blender, combine all of the ingredients and blend on high speed for 45 seconds. Pour the mixture through a nut-milk bag or fine-mesh sieve into a tall glass.
Makes 1 serving

ALMOND MILK

Here is a simple almond milk base for other recipes. Or, you can enjoy it on its own with a little stevia added to taste.

2 cups (16 fl oz/500 ml) filtered water

½ cup (2½ oz/75 g) Soaked Almonds (page 168)

⅛ teaspoon ground cinnamon

¼ teaspoon alcohol-free vanilla extract

In a blender, combine all of the ingredients and blend on high speed for 45 seconds. Pour the mixture through a nut-milk bag or fine-mesh sieve.

Makes about 2 cups (16 fl oz/500 ml)

CACAO-ALMOND MILK

Who didn't love chocolate milk as a kid? This is my healthy, vegan version, which is rich in antioxidants and magnesium. It's perhaps more appealing than the childhood version for adults, but your kids will never know the difference.

2 cups (16 fl oz/500 ml) water

½ cup (2½ oz/75 g) Soaked Almonds (page 168)

5 Medjool dates, pitted and coarsely chopped

3 tablespoons raw cacao powder

¼ teaspoon alcohol-free vanilla extract

¼ teaspoon ground cinnamon

In a blender, combine all of the ingredients and blend on high speed for 45 seconds. Pour the mixture through a nut-milk bag or fine-mesh sieve into a tall glass.

Makes 1 serving

ORANGE-CARROT-ALMOND DREAMSICLE

One of my all-time favorite nut milks, this combo is not only beautiful to look at but also a dream to drink.

½ cup (4 fl oz/125 ml) carrot juice

½ cup (4 fl oz/125 ml) fresh orange juice

½ cup (4 fl oz/125 ml) Almond Milk (above)

Pour the carrot and orange juices into a tall glass. Slowly pour the almond milk into the glass.

Makes 1 serving

NO-EGG NOG

Here is the perfect beverage for anyone who craves the Christmas treat but wishes to skip the sugar, dairy, and alcohol. This drink is a favorite in Urban Remedy stores around the holidays.

1 cup (8 fl oz/250 ml) Cashew Milk (page 141)

1 cup (8 fl oz/250 ml) Almond Milk (left)

3 Medjool dates, pitted and coarsely chopped

1 tablespoon traditional vanilla extract

¼ teaspoon ground cinnamon

¼ teaspoon freshly grated nutmeg

In a blender, combine all of the ingredients and blend on high speed for 45 seconds. Pour into a tall glass.

Makes 1 serving

MACA HEMP MILK

This is a milk to boost your libido! Both the Peruvian root maca and the hemp are believed by some to be effective aphrodisiacs.

½ cup (4 oz/125 g) shelled hemp seeds

1½ cups (12 fl oz/375 ml) filtered water

2 tablespoons maple syrup, or 20 drops liquid stevia

1 teaspoon alcohol-free vanilla extract

½ teaspoon maca powder

Pinch of sea salt

In a blender, combine all of the ingredients and blend on high speed for 45 seconds. Pour into a tall glass.

Makes 1 serving

Orange-Carrot-Almond Dreamsicle,
opposite page

Blueberry-Goji-Açai Smoothie,
opposite page

SMOOTHIES

Smoothies are tasty and filling, and drinking them is a great way to enjoy a nutrition-packed meal in a glass. My perfect smoothie includes antioxidants, protein, healthy fats, and a host of other nutrients. Berries, kale, avocado, chia seeds, and nut milks are some of my favorite smoothie additions.

LIME-AVOCADO BRAIN FOOD SMOOTHIE

This luscious smoothie is rich in healthy omega-3s and monounsaturated fats that are excellent for the brain and heart health as well as for blood sugar balance. This smoothie is so thick you can almost eat it with a spoon. For an extra treat, sprinkle the smoothie with a little French grey sea salt.

¼ cup (2 fl oz/60 ml) filtered water

½ avocado

1 teaspoon coconut oil

1½ cups (12 fl oz/375 ml) Almond Milk (page 142)

15 drops liquid stevia or 2 tablespoons coconut palm sugar

1 tablespoon alcohol-free vanilla extract

In a blender, combine all of the ingredients and blend on high speed for 45 seconds. The smoothie will be thick. Pour into a tall glass.

Makes 1 serving

CHOCO-BANANA SMOOTHIE

Kids love this smoothie because it tastes like a milk shake. Adults love it because it is a guilt-free treat. Bananas have been shown to lower blood pressure.

1½ cups (12 fl oz/375 ml) Almond Milk (page 142)

1½ frozen peeled bananas

2 tablespoons raw cacao powder

¼ teaspoon ground cinnamon

1 tablespoon chia seeds

In a blender, combine all of the ingredients and blend on high speed for 45 seconds. The smoothie should be smooth and thick. Pour into a tall glass.

Makes 1 serving

PROTEIN POWER SMOOTHIE

This smoothie packs that extra protein punch with plant-based proteins.

1½ cups (12 fl oz/375 ml) Almond Milk (page 142)

2 tablespoons shelled hemp seeds

1 tablespoon spirulina powder

1 frozen peeled banana

7 drops liquid stevia, or 5 Medjool dates, pitted and coarsely chopped

In a blender, combine all of the ingredients and blend on high speed for 45 seconds. The smoothie should be smooth and thick. Pour into a tall glass.

Makes 1 serving

BLUEBERRY-GOJI-AÇAI SMOOTHIE

Rich in antioxidants, this colorful smoothie is great for fighting the signs of aging.

1½ cups (12 fl oz/375 ml) Almond Milk (page 142)

½ cup (2 oz/60 g) frozen blueberries

½ packet (1.75 oz/50 g) unsweetened açai purée

2 tablespoons dried goji berries

½ teaspoon ground cinnamon

In a blender, combine all of the ingredients and blend on high speed for 45 seconds. The smoothie should be smooth and thick. Pour into a tall glass.

Makes 1 serving

In addition to what you see here, look for another smoothie in the 4-day Cleanse on page 75.

RASPBERRY SUPERFOOD SMOOTHIE

Raspberries are chock-full of antioxidants, which are great for combating the signs of aging and inflammation. Hemp is added for its healthy oils and protein. Chia promotes sustained energy and delivers omega-3s. Spinach is rich in chlorophyll and has cleansing benefits.

1 cup (8 fl oz/250 ml) Almond Milk (page 142)

1 cup (4 oz/125 g) frozen raspberries

½ cup (3 oz/90 g) chia gel (page 75)

1 tablespoon shelled hemp seeds

1 teaspoon virgin coconut oil

10 drops stevia or 2 tablespoons coconut palm sugar

½ cup (½ oz/15 g) spinach

In a blender, combine all of the ingredients and blend on high speed for 45 seconds. The smoothie should be smooth and thick. Pour into a tall glass.

Makes 1 serving

MANGO-GREEN-CHIA SMOOTHIE

Energizing chia and antioxidant-rich mango will help jump start your day.

1½ cups (12 fl oz/375 ml) water

1 cup (5 oz/155 g) frozen mango

1 frozen peeled banana

3 kale leaves, stemmed

1 tablespoon chia seeds

6 drops liquid stevia

In a blender, combine the water, mango, banana, kale, chia seeds, and stevia and blend on high speed until smooth, about 45 seconds. Pour into a tall glass.

Makes 1 serving

CHAI-SPICE SHAKE

Loaded with anti-inflammatory properties, this creamy shake boasts the fragrance of garam masala and the natural sweetness of dates.

1½ cups (12 fl oz/375 ml) Cashew Milk (page 141)

½ cup (2 oz/60 g) unsweetened shredded dried coconut

4 Medjool dates, pitted and coarsely chopped

½ teaspoon garam masala

3 tablespoons raw protein powder (I recommend Sunwarrior brand)

In a blender, combine all of the ingredients and blend on high speed for 45 seconds. The smoothie should be smooth and thick. Pour into a tall glass.

Makes 1 serving

MINT–CACAO CHIP SMOOTHIE

A day before you plan to enjoy this smoothie, peel the bananas, seal them in a zippered plastic freezer bag, and pop them into the freezer. That way, you'll be ready to make this delicious drink. I recommend freezing a bunch of bananas at the same time, so you always have some on hand for smoothies. Raw cacao is considered a super antioxidant. Both cinnamon and chia help balance blood sugar.

1½ cups (12 fl oz/375 ml) Almond Milk (page 142), or more if needed

1½ frozen peeled bananas

1½ cups (1½ oz/45 g) baby spinach leaves

Leaves from 1½ bunches fresh mint

1 tablespoon alcohol-free vanilla extract

1 teaspoon ground cinnamon

3 tablespoons raw cacao nibs

Liquid stevia, for sweetening (optional)

In a blender, combine the almond milk, bananas, spinach, mint, vanilla, and cinnamon and blend on high speed until the mixture is smooth, about 45 seconds. Then add the cacao nibs and blend for 20 seconds, to break up the nibs and add texture. Pour into a tall glass. Sweeten with stevia to taste, if desired.

Makes 1 serving

Mint Cacao Chip Smoothie,
opposite page

Avocado, Tomato, and Sprout
Salad, opposite page

SALADS AND SOUPS

Eating mostly plant-based foods is one of the best things you can do your health. Plants contain valuable phytonutrients, fiber, antioxidants, vitamins, and minerals. You can eat these salads and soups for lunch or dinner. I tried to make them supereasy to assemble for people with busy schedules.

ROASTED BUTTERNUT AND POMEGRANATE SALAD

The bright orange of the butternut combined with the beautiful tones of pomegranate seeds make this salad not only delicious but a dish to impress guests.

½ small butternut squash, peeled, seeded, and cut into 1-inch (2.5-cm) cubes

3 cups (3 oz/90 g) chopped romaine lettuce

1 cup (3 oz/90 g) very finely shredded purple cabbage

Seeds of ½ ripe pomegranate

FOR THE DRESSING

½ clove garlic, passed through a garlic press

¼ teaspoon sea salt

1 tablespoon extra-virgin olive oil

1 tablespoon cider vinegar

Preheat the oven to 350°F (180°C). Spread the squash cubes on a rimmed baking sheet and roast until tender, about 25 minutes. Remove from the oven and let cool.

To make the salad, in a bowl, combine the lettuce, cabbage, and pomegranate seeds, toss to mix well, then top with the cooled squash.

To make the dressing, in a small bowl, stir together the garlic, salt, oil, and vinegar, mixing well. Drizzle the dressing over the salad and toss to coat evenly.

Makes 1 serving

AVOCADO, TOMATO, AND SPROUT SALAD

Sunflower sprouts are a complete source of protein and rich in health-promoting enzymes.

3 cups (6 oz/185 g) sunflower sprouts

1 large heirloom tomato, cut into 1-inch (2.5-cm) pieces

1 avocado, halved, pitted, peeled, and cut into 1-inch (2.5-cm) pieces

2 tablespoons cider vinegar

1 teaspoon Himalayan pink salt

In a bowl, combine the sprouts, tomato, and avocado. Drizzle with the vinegar, sprinkle with the salt, and stir and toss to mix well. The avocado will soften as you mix the ingredients, coating the tomato and sprouts with an oil-free dressing.

Makes 1 serving

MIXED HERB SALAD

This simple yet beautiful blend of herbs makes for a delicious and nutritious salad.

2 cups mixed salad greens

⅓ cup (½ oz/15 g) chopped fresh mint

4 fresh basil leaves, coarsely chopped

¼ cup (¼ oz/7 g) fresh cilantro leaves

2 tablespoons shelled hemp seeds

FOR THE DRESSING

2 teaspoons extra-virgin olive oil

¼ teaspoon sea salt

2 teaspoons cider vinegar

To make the salad, in a bowl, combine the greens, mint, basil, cilantro, and hemp seeds and toss to mix.

To make the dressing, in a small bowl, stir together the oil, salt, and vinegar, mixing well.

Drizzle the dressing over the salad and toss to coat evenly.

Makes 1 serving

In addition to what you see here, look for other salads and soups in the 4-day cleanse on pages 58–94.

CUCUMBER-AVOCADO-CILANTRO SALAD

Here, the cucumber flushes the body, while the avocado provides essential omega-3 fatty acids. This is a great light and refreshing summertime salad. Cilantro has been shown to contain properties that remove heavy metal buildup in the body. Tomatoes are rich in beta-carotene and lycopene, which have been shown to have anti-cancer benefits.

1 cucumber, halved lengthwise, seeded, and cut into 1-inch (2.5-cm) cubes

1 cup (6 oz/185 g) cherry tomatoes, halved

1 avocado, halved, pitted, peeled, and cut into 1-inch (2.5-cm) cubes

½ bunch fresh cilantro, coarsely chopped

1 red bell pepper, seeded and chopped

FOR THE DRESSING

1 small clove garlic, passed through a garlic press

½ teaspoon sea salt

1 tablespoon extra-virgin olive oil

Pinch of freshly ground black pepper

1 tablespoon cider vinegar

To make the salad, in a bowl, combine the cucumber, tomatoes, avocado, cilantro, and bell pepper; toss to mix.

To make the dressing in a small bowl, stir together the garlic, salt, oil, pepper, and vinegar, mixing well. Drizzle the dressing over the salad and toss to coat evenly.

Makes 1 serving

FERMENTED SALAD

Fermented foods are some of the best foods for your gut health because they populate your intestinal system with healthy bacteria. This salad must sit for 3 days before it can be eaten, so plan ahead.

½ head small head napa cabbage, thinly sliced, plus 1 large leaf

1 red bell pepper, seeded and finely chopped

1 carrot, thinly sliced

½ teaspoon peeled and grated fresh ginger

1 teaspoon Himalayan pink salt

Brine solution of 3 cups (24 fl oz/750 ml) distilled water and 1 tablespoon sea salt

In a large bowl, combine the sliced cabbage, bell pepper, carrot, ginger, and salt and toss to mix. Let sit for 5 minutes to allow the vegetables to release some moisture. Then, using your hands, squeeze the vegetable mixture thoroughly to release as much excess moisture as possible.

Transfer the vegetable mixture to a 1 qt (32 fl oz/1 l) canning jar. Lay the whole cabbage leaf on top of the mixture. Pour enough of the brine solution into the jar to just cover the leaf. Put the jar in a dry place with a temperature of 75°F (24°C) and let it stand, undisturbed, for 3 days.

The salad is now ready to eat. To store, cap the jar tightly and refrigerate. It will keep for up to about 2 weeks.
Makes about 8 servings

SPINACH-HEMP-CURRANT SALAD

Flaxseed oil is rich in lignans (which are great for treating menopausal symptoms), antioxidants, and essential omega-3 fatty acids. The currants give the salad a nice sweet surprise.

3 cups (3 oz/90 g) loosely packed baby spinach leaves

2 tablespoons dried currants

1 tablespoon shelled hemp seeds

FOR THE DRESSING

½ clove garlic, passed through a garlic press

¼ teaspoon sea salt

2 teaspoons extra-virgin olive oil

2 teaspoons unfiltered flaxseed oil

1 tablespoon fresh Meyer lemon juice

To make the salad, in a bowl, combine the spinach, currants, and hemp seeds and toss to mix well.

To make the dressing, in a small bowl, stir together the garlic, salt, both oils, and the lemon juice, mixing well.

Drizzle the dressing over the salad and toss to coat evenly.
Makes 1 serving

Roasted Butternut and
Pomegranate Salad, page 149

Asian Kale Salad, page 77

KALE VEGAN CAESAR

The flavors in this Caesar dressing are remarkably satisfying, and when you combine the dressing with kale, you have a salad that fills you up and leaves you feeling great. If you prefer a more traditional Caesar, you can trade out the kale for romaine lettuce, or you can use of a mix of kale and romaine.

1 bunch Lacinato kale, stems removed, finely chopped

FOR THE DRESSING

1 large clove garlic, passed through a garlic press

½ teaspoon sea salt

2 tablespoons extra-virgin olive oil

2 teaspoons nutritional yeast

½ teaspoon gluten-free tamari

¼ teaspoon dry mustard

2 teaspoons fresh lemon juice

1 teaspoon cider vinegar

1 tablespoon capers

Put the kale in a bowl. To make the dressing, in a small bowl, combine the garlic and salt and mix well. Add the oil, yeast, tamari, mustard, lemon juice, vinegar, and capers to the garlic-salt mixture and again mix well. Drizzle the dressing over the kale and toss to coat evenly.
Makes 1 serving

TRICOLOR SLAW

This beautiful blend of cabbage and kale is great for your digestion and for keeping your GI tract healthy. I have used a hefty measure of sesame seeds and oil, which are rich in minerals like copper and magnesium and benefit the yin (fluids of the body) to help reduce dryness. The seeds are also believed to ease the symptoms of arthritis.

¼ head purple cabbage, finely shredded

¼ head napa cabbage, finely shredded

½ bunch Lacinato kale, finely chopped

2 carrots, grated

½ red bell pepper, seeded and cut into julienne

¼ bunch fresh cilantro, chopped

¼ cup (1¼ oz/35 g) raw sesame seeds

FOR THE DRESSING

2 tablespoons soy-free miso

2 tablespoons cold-pressed sesame oil

1 tablespoon cold-pressed flax oil

2 tablespoons cider vinegar

1 tablespoon coconut palm sugar or maple syrup

1 teaspoon peeled and finely chopped fresh ginger

½ clove garlic, minced

To make the salad, in a bowl, combine the purple and napa cabbages, kale, carrots, bell pepper, cilantro, and sesame seeds and toss to mix.

To make the dressing, in a small bowl, whisk together the miso, sesame and flax oils, vinegar, sugar, ginger, and garlic.

Drizzle the dressing over the salad and toss to coat evenly.
Makes 1 serving

MEDICINAL MISO SOUP

When you feel a cold or the flu coming on, make this soup for yourself. The miso builds the good bacteria in your intestinal tract for a stronger immune system. The green onions, or *cong bai*, are spicy and warming. They're great for inducing sweating and relieving the symptoms of colds and flu. Fresh ginger, or *sheng giang*, is also spicy and warm, so it's good to eat when you have a cold, cough, or flulike symptoms.

3 cups Alkalizing Mineral Broth (page 64) or filtered water

1-inch (2.5-cm) knob fresh ginger

2 tablespoons soy-free miso

3 green onions, white parts and about 1 inch (2.5 cm) of the green parts, chopped

In a saucepan, bring the broth and ginger to a boil. Remove from the heat and dissolve the miso in the warm broth. Top with the green onions and let sit for a few minutes before eating.
Makes 1 serving

GAZPACHO

Chock-full of detoxifying ingredients, this summer soup is refreshing and delicious. Tomatoes are a rich source of antioxidants, supporting heart and bone health. They also contain high amounts of lycopene, which has shown anticancer benefits. For the best flavor and maximum nutrient concentration, run tomatoes and celery through your juicer to make the fresh juice.

1½ cups (12 fl oz/375 ml) fresh tomato juice

¼ cup (2 fl oz/60 ml) fresh celery juice

¼ cup (2 fl oz/60 ml) cider vinegar

2 large heirloom tomatoes, chopped

1 cucumber, peeled and chopped

1 red bell pepper, seeded and chopped

½ cup (½ oz/15 g) fresh cilantro leaves

1 teaspoon sea salt

2 tablespoons extra-virgin olive oil

FOR THE TOPPINGS

¼ cup (¼ oz/7 g) fresh cilantro leaves, chopped

¼ cup (1½ oz/45 g) chopped cherry tomatoes

Extra-virgin olive oil, for drizzling

Pinch of sea salt

To make the soup, in a blender, combine the tomato juice, celery juice, vinegar, heirloom tomatoes, cucumber, bell pepper, cilantro, salt, and oil and blend on high speed until smooth.

Pour the soup into a bowl (or bowls) and top with the cilantro, tomatoes, a drizzle of oil, and the salt.

Makes 1–2 servings

In addition to what you see here, look for other meal ideas in the 4-day cleanse on pages 58–94.

MAIN COURSES

These recipes are satisfying enough to serve at any meal and boast great texture, flavor, and overall appeal. The fact that they are so delicious belies the fact that they are abundantly healthy.

RAW LASAGNE

My half-Italian side loves this dish, as it fulfills all my lasagne cravings without consuming any lymph system–clogging dairy or carb-laden noodles.

FOR THE CASHEW RICOTTA

1 cup (5½ oz/170 g) cashews, soaked in filtered water to cover for 2 hours, drained, and rinsed

1 tablespoon fresh lemon juice

1 tablespoon nutritional yeast

1 small clove garlic

⅓ cup (3 fl oz/80 ml) filtered water

½ teaspoon Himalayan pink salt

⅛ teaspoon freshly ground black pepper

FOR THE TOMATO SAUCE

2 cups (6 oz/185 g) dry-packed sun-dried tomatoes, soaked in 3 cups (24 fl oz/750 ml) water for 5 hours and drained, with water reserved

7 fresh basil leaves

1 clove garlic, minced

¼ cup (2 fl oz/60 ml) extra-virgin olive oil

1 teaspoon sea salt

½ teaspoon coconut palm sugar

2 zucchini, each about 6 inches (15 cm) long

2 large heirloom tomatoes

Large handful fresh basil leaves

To make the cashew ricotta, in a blender, combine all of the ingredients and blend on high speed for about 30 seconds. The mixture should be smooth and quite thick. You can add a little more water if it seems too thick. Transfer to a bowl, cover, and refrigerate until it firms up, about 15 minutes. It should be the consistency of real ricotta cheese.

To make the tomato sauce, in a clean blender, combine the soaked tomatoes, 2 cups (16 fl oz/500 ml) of the soaking water, the basil, garlic, oil, salt, and sugar and process

Raw Lasagne, opposite page

Vegetable Plate with Fried
Chickpeas and Roasted
Tomato, page 158

until smooth. If the sauce seems too thick, add more of the soaking water until a nice consistency is achieved.

Using a mandoline, cut the zucchini into wide ribbons. Cut the tomatoes crosswise into slices ¼ inch (6 mm) thick.

To assemble the lasagne, on a platter, layer one-third of the zucchini slices. Spread one-third of the tomato sauce evenly over the zucchini layer, then spread one-third of the cashew ricotta over the tomato sauce. Top with a few basil leaves and one-third of the tomato slices. Repeat the layers twice, ending with tomato slices. Top with additional basil leaves. Cover and refrigerate uneaten portions for up to 3 days.

Makes 4 servings.

PAD THAI VEGETABLE NOODLES

A Thai classic made with plant-based ingredients, this dish is a bit time-consuming, but worth the effort. Ginger supports digestion and you get a plethora of healing phytonutrients from the zucchini, daikon, carrots, red pepper, and herbs.

1 large zucchini, about 6 inches (15 cm) long

1 large daikon radish

2 large carrots, cut into julienne

1 red bell pepper, seeded and cut into julienne

¼ cup (⅓ oz/10 g) chopped fresh cilantro

¼ cup (⅓ oz/10 g) chopped fresh basil

FOR THE SAUCE

2 tablespoons almond butter

½ cup (4 fl oz/125 ml) fresh lime juice

5 fresh basil leaves

1-inch (2.5-cm) knob fresh ginger

¼ cup (¾ oz/20 g) shredded raw coconut, soaked in ½ cup (4 fl oz/125 ml) filtered water for 2 hours, then puréed

¼ jalapeño chile

1 tablespoon gluten-free tamari

1 clove garlic

1 tablespoon coconut palm sugar

¼ cup (1¼ oz/35 g) chopped Soaked Almonds (page 168)

2 tablespoons raw sesame seeds

Using a spiral vegetable cutter, cut the zucchini, followed by the daikon, into noodles. Transfer the noodles to a large bowl. Add the carrots, bell pepper, cilantro, and basil and toss to combine.

To make the sauce, in a blender, combine all of the ingredients and blend on high speed until smooth.

Drizzle the sauce over the noodle mixture and toss to coat evenly. Sprinkle with the almonds and sesame seeds.

Makes 1 serving

VEGAN SUSHI WITH JICAMA RICE

I love sushi. This recipe will satisfy your sushi craving without the concerns that sometimes come up about eating fish these days.

FOR THE DIPPING SAUCE

¼ cup (2 fl oz/60 ml) rice vinegar

1 tablespoon gluten-free tamari

1-inch (2.5-cm) knob peeled and minced fresh ginger

1 small fresh red chile, minced

½ teaspoon coconut palm sugar

FOR THE SUSHI RICE

1½ cups (6 oz/185 g) chopped jicama (1-inch/2.5-cm pieces)

2 tablespoons raw sesame seeds

2 tablespoons rice vinegar

¼ teaspoon sea salt

¼ teaspoon coconut palm sugar

2 tablespoons alfalfa sprouts

¼ avocado, peeled and cut lengthwise into strips

3 sheets raw nori, about 7½ by 8 inches (19 by 20 cm)

¼ cucumber, halved lengthwise, seeded, and cut into 1-inch (2.5-cm) chunks

2 tablespoons red bell pepper pieces (1-inch/2.5-cm pieces)

To make the dipping sauce, in a small bowl, stir together all of the ingredients, mixing well. Set aside for 1 hour to allow the flavors to blend.

To make the sushi rice, in a food processor, combine all of the ingredients and pulse until the mixture is the texture of white rice. Transfer to a fine-mesh sieve, place over a bowl, and let stand for 1 hour to drain any excess moisture.

Place a nori sheet, shiny side down, on the work surface in front of you. Spread ½ cup (2½ oz/75 g) of the sushi rice on the half of the nori sheet closest to you, leaving 2 inches (5 cm) of the far side of the sheet uncovered, spreading it thinly and evenly. Starting about 1 inch (2.5 cm) in from the edge closest to you, arrange the avocado, cucumber, bell pepper, and sprouts in tightly arranged rows next to one another on the rice mixture.

Lift the edge of the nori sheet closest to you up and over the filling ingredients and then roll away from you, applying even, steady pressure to form a snug, uniform roll. Before you reach the uncovered nori, lightly dampen the edge of it with water and then continue to roll, sealing the dampened edge to the roll.

Using a sharp knife, cut the roll crosswise into 2-inch (5-cm) pieces and then arrange the pieces on a plate. Repeat with the remaining nori sheets to make 2 more rolls, cutting them into pieces and adding to the plate. Accompany with the dipping sauce.

Makes 1 serving

VEGETABLE PLATE WITH FRIED CHICKPEAS AND ROASTED TOMATO

Dandelion greens, which are prized for their ability to detoxify the liver and stomach, are characteristically bitter. Look for younger greens, as they are less bitter. Or, to lessen the sharp flavor, you can boil the greens for 1 minute to wilt them. The chickpeas will take about 2 days to sprout, so you'll need to plan ahead for this dish.

½ cup (3½ oz/105 g) dried chickpeas, sprouted (directions follow)

1 cup (6 oz/185 g) cherry tomatoes, or 4 plum tomatoes, halved

1 tablespoon coconut oil

¼ teaspoon sea salt

¼ cup (2 fl oz/60 ml) filtered water

1 bunch dandelion greens, stemmed, leaves torn into large pieces

3 cups (3 oz/90 g) spinach leaves

2–3 tablespoons fresh lemon juice

1 teaspoon ground cumin

To make the sprouted chickpeas, rinse them under running cold water, then transfer to a widemouthed canning jar or similar container. Add filtered water to cover the chickpeas, then cover the container with cheesecloth and secure it in place with a rubber band. Place the jar in a cool place and let the chickpeas soak for 24 hours.

Drain off the water from the chickpeas through the cheesecloth, then drain and rinse them two times. Select a room-temperature spot out of sunlight, and place the jar on its side on a kitchen towel, with the bottom of the jar propped up so any excess water can drain off. Leave the jar in that spot for 36–48 hours, rinsing and draining the chickpeas once every 8–12 hours. At this point, the sprouted tails should be about ¼ inch (6 mm) long. Rinse and drain the chickpeas one more time, then allow the sprouted chickpeas to air-dry. To store the sprouted chickpeas, transfer them to a container and refrigerate for up to 5 days.

Preheat the oven to 350°F (180°C). Put the tomatoes on a rimmed baking sheet, drizzle with the oil, sprinkle with the salt, and toss to coat evenly. Spread the tomatoes on the baking sheet and roast until they are soft and blistered, about 25 minutes. Transfer to a plate.

In a saucepan, combine the water, dandelion, and spinach over medium heat and cook, stirring occasionally, just until wilted, about 4 minutes. Set the greens on the plate alongside the tomatoes.

Wipe out the saucepan, drying it well, then add the chickpeas, lemon juice, and cumin and fry over low heat until all of the liquid has evaporated. Transfer the chickpeas to the plate, setting them next to the greens.

Makes 1 serving

Beet and Zucchini Carpaccio
with Pine Nuts, page 162

Steamed Asparagus with Chopped Egg, Tarragon, and Lemon, opposite page

QUINOA TABBOULEH

This gluten-free take on tabbouleh is light and refreshing. Quinoa is a true food superstar. It is alkaline forming, high in protein and essential fatty acids and minerals, and free of gluten. In Chinese medicine, quinoa supports kidney function and is slightly warming.

2 cups (16 fl oz/500 ml) filtered water

1 cup (5½ oz/170 g) quinoa (any color), well rinsed

1 large cucumber, halved lengthwise, seeded, and finely diced

2 cups (12 oz/375 g) cherry tomatoes, halved

⅔ cup (1 oz/30 g) chopped fresh flat-leaf parsley

½ cup (¾ oz/20 g) chopped fresh mint

3 tablespoons, fresh lemon juice

2 tablespoons extra-virgin olive oil

1 clove garlic, minced

½ teaspoon sea salt or Himalayan pink salt

⅛ teaspoon freshly ground black pepper

To cook the quinoa, in a small saucepan, bring the water to a boil. Add the quinoa, reduce the heat to low, cover, and cook until the water has been absorbed and the quinoa is fluffy, 15–20 minutes. Remove from the heat, uncover, and fluff with a fork. Transfer to a bowl and let cool.

Add the cucumber, tomatoes, parsley, mint, lemon juice, oil, garlic, salt, and pepper to the cooled quinoa and stir and toss to mix well. Cover and refrigerate unused portions for up to 4 days.

Makes 4 servings

SIDE DISHES

If you want a nourishing side dish to go along with your main meal, turn to these nutrient-packed recipes. Many of these tasty options can also stand in as a light meal on their own.

STEAMED ASPARAGUS WITH CHOPPED EGG, TARRAGON, AND LEMON

If you have eaten a high-fat diet in the past, the lemon juice here will be good for you because of its cleansing ability. The asparagus, which is warming, a natural diuretic, and benefits the kidneys, is also a healthful addition to your diet.

1 bunch asparagus, tough ends trimmed

2 organic eggs from pastured hens

3 tablespoons chopped fresh tarragon

1 tablespoon fresh lemon juice

2 teaspoons extra-virgin olive oil

½ teaspoon sea salt

Pour filtered water to a depth of 3 inches (7.5 cm) into the base of a steamer and bring to a boil. Arrange the asparagus on the steamer rack, cover, and steam until tender but still crunchy, 4–6 minutes.

Meanwhile, put the eggs in a saucepan, add filtered water to cover, and place over high heat. As soon as the water reaches a brisk simmer, turn off the heat. Let the eggs stand in the water for 4½ minutes. The eggs should be soft boiled. Immediately remove the pan from the heat and place under cold running water until the eggs are cool enough to handle. Peel the eggs and chop them.

In a bowl, combine the warm asparagus, tarragon, lemon juice, oil, and salt and toss to mix well. Transfer to a platter and top with the chopped eggs.

Makes 2 servings

CAULIFLOWER MASH WITH KALE AND GARLIC

Both cabbage and kale are regarded as cancer-fighting foods and both garlic and coconut boost the immune system, which makes this simple, tasty dish a healthful choice for lunch or supper.

4 cups (32 fl oz/1 l) filtered water

1 small head cauliflower, cut into florets

1 tablespoon coconut oil

1 small clove garlic

½ teaspoon sea salt

½ cup (1½ oz/45 g) finely shredded kale

In a saucepan, bring the water to a boil over high heat. Add the cauliflower, reduce the heat to low, and cook until soft, 6–8 minutes. Remove from the heat and drain the cauliflower, reserving the cooking water.

In a food processor, combine the warm cauliflower, oil, garlic, and salt and purée until smooth, adding a bit of the cooking water if needed for a good consistency.

Transfer the purée to a bowl, add the kale, and stir until the kale is wilted from the heat of the cauliflower.

Makes 2–3 servings

BEET AND ZUCCHINI CARPACCIO WITH PINE NUTS

I like the simplicity of this colorful dish. Plus, it celebrates the humble beet, which contributes to good liver health, oxygenates cells to increase stamina, calms the spirit, and supports normal blood pressure levels.

1 large beet

1 zucchini, about 5 inches (13 cm) long

Extra-virgin olive oil, for drizzling

1 teaspoon coarse sea salt

3 tablespoons raw pine nuts

Using a mandoline or a sharp knife, slice the beet and zucchini as thinly as possible.

Transfer the beet and zucchini slices to a plate, drizzle lightly with the oil, and toss to coat evenly. Sprinkle with the salt and pine nuts.

Makes 2–3 servings

DESSERTS

I have a pretty serious sweet tooth, but I find that desserts made with white flour and sugar make me feel poorly. The desserts that follow are made with plant-based ingredients that are rich in nutrients. I've worked hard to replicate the taste and texture of classic desserts made the traditional way, while retaining the healthful qualities in these raw desserts. My versions will leave you feeling satisfied and energized.

RAW CHOCOLATE MOUSSE WITH ALMOND CRÈME

Here is the ideal, no-guilt dessert for chocolate lovers. The base is avocado, which builds up the yin in your body to prevent dry skin, hair, and eyes. The generous measure of antioxidant-rich cacao fights off pesky free radicals that can age your skin. For a low-glycemic dessert, choose stevia over the dates and coconut palm sugar.

FOR THE MOUSSE

1 large ripe avocado

⅓ cup (1 oz/30 g) raw cacao powder

¼ cup (2 fl oz/60 ml) Almond Milk (page 142)

7 Medjool dates, pitted and coarsely chopped, or 2 teaspoons liquid stevia

1 teaspoon alcohol-free vanilla extract

¼ teaspoon ground cinnamon

FOR THE ALMOND CRÈME

¼ cup Soaked Almonds (page 168)

2 tablespoons Almond Milk (page 142)

1 tablespoon coconut palm sugar, or ½ teaspoon liquid stevia

Pinch of sea salt

To make the mousse, add all of the ingredients to a blender and blend for about 1 minute, until creamy. Divide the mixture among 2 individual custard cups.

To make the almond crème, in a clean blender, combine all of the ingredients and blend on high speed until smooth.

Raw Chocolate Mousse with
Almond Crème, opposite page

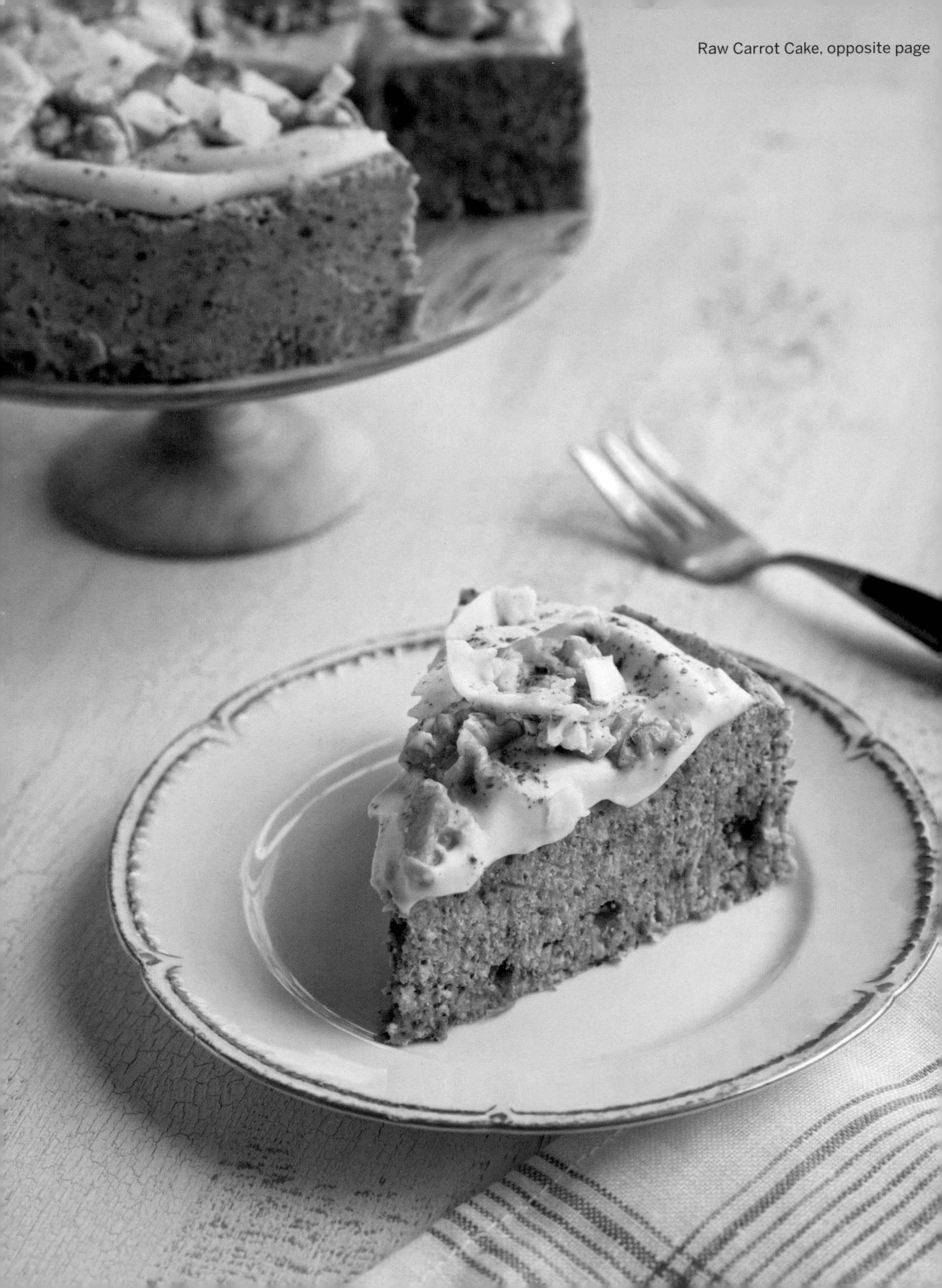

Raw Carrot Cake, opposite page

Top each mousse cup with a large dollop of the almond crème, cover, and refrigerate until firm, about 2 hours.

Makes 2 servings

RAW CRÈME CARAMEL

One day I had too many soaked cashews on hand, and voilà, this crème caramel was born. It is now a favorite Urban Remedy offering. The combination of sweet, salty, and creamy is irresistible.

- 1 cup (5 oz/155 g) Soaked Cashews (page 168)
- ¼ cup (2 oz/60 g) coconut palm sugar
- 1 tablespoon alcohol-free vanilla extract
- 1 tablespoon coconut oil
- ¼ cup (2 oz/60 g) chopped or slivered almonds
- Pinch of sea salt

In a blender, combine the cashews, sugar, vanilla, and coconut oil and blend on high speed until smooth. Divide the mixture between 2 custard cups. Mix the chopped almonds with the salt and sprinkle on top of each dessert.

Makes 2 servings

BUTTERNUT CHIA PUDDING

Butternut squash is used in Chinese medicine to balance blood sugar levels and alleviate lung issues. It is also high in vitamin A, which contributes to a healthy immune system.

- 1 cup (4½ oz/140 g) peeled and cubed butternut squash
- 5 Medjool dates, pitted and coarsely chopped
- ¼ cup (2 fl oz/60 ml) coconut oil
- ⅓ cup (3½ oz/105 g) pure maple syrup
- 1 tablespoon pumpkin pie spice
- 1 tablespoon chia seeds
- ½ cup (4 fl oz/125 ml) Almond Milk (page 142)

In a blender, combine all of the ingredients and blend on high speed until smooth. Divide the mixture between 2 individual custard cups, cover, and refrigerate for about 2 hours.

Makes 2 servings

CREAMY ORANGE PUDDING

Rich in vitamins C and A, orange juice is cooling and sweet and helps alleviate sluggish digestion.

- ½ cup (2¾ oz/80 g) Soaked Cashews (page 168)
- 2 cups (16 fl oz/500 ml) fresh orange juice
- 1 tablespoon pure maple syrup, or ½ teaspoon liquid stevia
- 3 tablespoons chia seeds
- 1 tablespoon alcohol-free vanilla extract
- Orange segments, for serving

Put the cashews in a food processor. With the machine running, slowly add a few tablespoons of the orange juice until a pudding-like texture forms. Slowly add the remaining orange juice, maple syrup, and vanilla and blend until fully incorporated. Add the chia seeds and process until well mixed. Divide the mixture between 2 small custard cups, cover, and refrigerate overnight. Serve chilled, topped with fresh orange segments.

Makes 2 servings

RAW CARROT CAKE

Carrots are full of beta-carotene, which contributes to good vision and a healthy immune system. Here they make a satisfying dessert that tastes just like carrot cake but without the gluten and white sugar.

FOR THE CAKE
- 4 large carrots, finely grated
- 3 cups (11 oz/345 g) almond flour
- 10–14 Medjool dates, pitted and coarsely chopped
- 1 cup (4 oz/125 g) unsweetened shredded dried coconut
- 1 teaspoon ground cinnamon
- ½ cup (2 oz/60 g) walnuts
- 2 tablespoons coconut oil

FOR THE FROSTING
- 1 cup (5½ oz/170 g) Soaked Cashews (page 168)
- 2 tablespoons Almond Milk (page 142)
- 1 tablespoon fresh lemon juice
- 2 tablespoons coconut oil, melted
- 1 tablespoon alcohol-free vanilla extract
- ¼ cup (2½ oz/75 g) date syrup or pure maple syrup
- Ground cinnamon, for garnish

To make the cake, in a food processor, combine all of the ingredients and process until thoroughly mixed and soft. Remove the mixture from the processor and press into a 6-inch (15-cm) cake pan.

To make the frosting, in a blender, combine all of the ingredients and blend on high speed until smooth.

Spread the frosting over the top of the cake and garnish with a light dusting of cinnamon. Cover and refrigerate until set, 30–60 minutes.

Makes 4–6 servings

BERRIES WITH ALMOND CRÈME

This creamy, dreamy dessert takes minutes to make. Raspberries and blueberries are loaded with antioxidants and have low glycemic value. Opt for stevia over the date or maple syrup to keep it low on the glycemic scale.

FOR THE ALMOND CRÈME
1 cup (5½ oz/170 g) Soaked Almonds (page 168)

½ cup (4 fl oz/125 ml) filtered water

1 tablespoon coconut oil

1 tablespoon date syrup or pure maple syrup, or 1 dropperful of liquid stevia

½ cup (2 oz/60 g) fresh raspberries

½ cup (2 oz/60 g) blueberries

To make the almond crème, in a blender, combine all of the ingredients and blend on high speed until smooth. If not serving immediately, cover and refrigerate until needed.

Divide half of the raspberries among 2 parfait glasses. Top each portion of berries with a large dollop of almond crème. Top the almond crème with half of the blueberries, and then top each portion of blueberries with another dollop of the almond crème. Repeat the layers with the remaining berries and almond crème. If you are not enjoying them right away, cover the parfaits and refrigerate for up to 3 days.

Makes 2 servings

SNACKS

Here are some superquick and healthy snacks your whole family will enjoy. I like to make these in big batches on the weekend so that I can grab them and go during the busy workweek.

ZUCCHINI CHIPS

Zucchini chips are a great alternative to store-bought corn chips. Serve them with Paul's Famous Guac (PAGE 168) and you'll never go back to deep-fried chips again.

1 large zucchini

1 tablespoon grapeseed oil

1 teaspoon Himalayan pink salt or sea salt

Preheat the oven to 225°F (110°C). Using a mandoline or sharp knife, cut the zucchini into slices ¼ inch (6 mm) thick. Pile the zucchini slices on a rimmed baking sheet. Drizzle with the oil, sprinkle with the salt, and toss to coat evenly. Arrange the slices in a single layer on the pan. Bake the slices until they are crisp, about 45 minutes. Remove from the oven and enjoy. Store any leftover chips in an airtight container at room temperature for up to 3 days.

Makes about 2 cups (2 oz/60 g)

KALE CHIPS

The kale chip craze is in full swing. Because most people don't have a dehydrator at home, here is a way to make the chips in your oven.

1 bunch Lacinato or curly kale, stems removed

2 tablespoons extra-virgin olive oil

1 teaspoon sea salt

Preheat the oven to 200°F (95°C). Pile the kale leaves on a rimmed baking sheet, then drizzle them with the oil, sprinkle with the salt, and toss to coat evenly. Arrange the leaves in a single layer on the pan. Bake the kale leaves until they are crisp, about 20 minutes. Remove from the oven and enjoy. Store any leftover chips in an airtight container at room temperature for up to 3 days.

Makes about 3 cups (3 oz/90 g)

FAUX CHEESE KALE CHIPS After removing the chips from the oven, sprinkle them with 2 tablespoons nutritional yeast and ¼ teaspoon ground turmeric.

SESAME KALE CHIPS Substitute 1 tablespoon cold-pressed sesame oil for 1 tablespoon of the olive oil. Toss the leaves with the oils, 1 tablespoon raw sesame seeds, 1 tablespoon gluten-free tamari, and 1 tablespoon coconut palm sugar before baking as directed.

PAUL'S FAMOUS GUAC

My BFF, Paul, makes the best guacamole I have ever eaten, so I talked him into sharing his secret recipe. Serve with Zucchini Chips **(PAGE 166)**.

- 1 ripe avocado
- 1 ripe tomato
- ¼ small Maui sweet onion
- ½ cup (4 fl oz/125 ml) fresh lime juice
- Himalayan pink salt

Halve, pit, and peel the avocado, then place in a bowl and mash with a fork. Halve the tomato crosswise, then grate the flesh on the large holes of a handheld grater, discarding the skin that is left behind. Grate the onion in the same way. Add the tomato and onion to the avocado and mix, then mix in the lime juice and the salt to taste.

Makes about 1½ cups (12 oz/375 g)

SUPERFOOD SEA SALT TRAIL MIX

This is a simple blend of superfoods rich in minerals and antioxidants. I always pack a batch when I am traveling or otherwise on the go. It keeps your blood sugar balanced and is easy to carry.

- 1 cup (5 oz/155 g) sunflower seeds
- 1 cup (5 oz/155 g) shelled pumpkin seeds
- ½ cup (4 oz/125 g) raw cacao nibs
- ½ cup (4 oz/125 g) raw sesame seeds
- ½ cup (4 oz/125 g) dried goji berries
- ¼ cup (1½ oz/45 g) golden raisins or dried currants
- ½ cup (1½ oz/45 g) dried coconut flakes
- ¼ teaspoon Himalayan pink salt

In a large bowl, stir and toss together all of the ingredients until well mixed. Transfer the mix to small zippered plastic bags to tote for low blood sugar moments.

Makes about 4½ cups (8 oz/250 g)

BERRIES AND NUTS

The simplest of all recipes, this low-glycemic combo is great when you are running out of the house and forget to eat. It will keep your blood sugar balanced.

- 1 cup (4 oz/125 g) fresh raspberries, blueberries, or blackberries, or a combination
- 1 cup (5½ oz/170 g) Soaked Almonds (below)

Put the berries and nuts in a bag or bowl and toss together. Enjoy as a snack.

Makes about 2 cups (10 oz/315 g)

SOAKED ALMONDS

Soaking almonds unlocks their health benefits. Many nuts contain enzyme inhibitors that protect them. The soaking process stimulates the germination process, which removes these inhibitors and makes the nuts even more nutritious and easy to digest.

- 1 cup (5½ oz/170 g) raw almonds
- 6 cups (48 fl oz/1.5 l) filtered water

In a glass bowl, combine the almonds and water and let stand at room temperature for 12 hours. Drain, rinse, and use right away, or refrigerate and use within 24 hours.

Makes about 1 cup (5½ oz/170 g)

SOAKED CASHEWS

Like with almonds, soaking cashews helps optimize the nutritional benefits that the nuts possess. Since cashews don't have a skin, the soaking time is less than for almonds.

- 1 cup (5½ oz/170 g) raw cashews
- 6 cups (48 fl oz/1.5 l) filtered water

In a glass bowl, combine the cashews and water and let stand at room temperature for 6 hours. Drain, rinse, and use right away or refrigerate and use within 24 hours.

Makes about 1 cup (5½ oz/170 g)

INDEX

BIBLIOGRAPHY

Pitchford, Paul. *Healing with Whole Foods,* 3 Rev Exp edition. Berkeley, CA: North Atlantic Books, November 5, 2002

Kaptchuck, Ted. *The Web That Has No Weaver: Understanding Chinese Medicine,* 2 edition. New York: McGraw-Hill, May 2, 2000

Beinfield, Harriet, and Korngold, Efrem. *Between Heaven and Earth: A Guide to Chinese Medicine.* New York: Ballantine Books, June 30, 1992

Maciocia, Giovanni. *The Foundations of Chinese Medicine: A Comprehensive Text for Acupuncturists and Herbalists.* Oxford, UK: Churchill Livingstone, September 18, 1989

Prousk, Jonathan and Hoffer, John. *Textbook of Integrative Clinical Nutrition.* Kingston, ON Canada: CCNM Press, February 10, 2013

All charts adapted with permission from McNease, Cathy and Dr. Ni, Mao Shing. *Basic Concepts of Chinese Nutrition and Medicine*: Foundation Concepts Manual, except for the Energetic Properties of common foods chart, which is adapted with permission from Integral Living Institute, Santa Monica, CA ©2001

weldonowen

1045 Sansome Street, Suite 100, San Francisco, CA 94111
www.weldonowen.com

**URBAN REMEDY
A WELDON OWEN PRODUCTION**

Copyright © 2014 Weldon Owen, Inc.

All rights reserved, including the right of
reproduction in whole or in part in any form.

This edition printed in 2014
10 9 8 7 6 5 4 3 2 1

Printed and bound by RR Donnelley in China

Library of Congress Cataloging-in-Publication
data is available

Weldon Owen is a division of
BONNIER

The program and advice presented in this book
does not guarantee results and should not be
used for diagnosing or treating a serious health
problem or disease. Consult your personal
health practitioner before starting any health
or wellness program. The client testimonials in
this book represent the anecdotal experiences;
individual experiences will vary.

PHOTO CREDITS
Melanie Acevedo, page 9
Shaun Sullivan, page 10

ISBN 13: 978-1-61628-814-3
ISBN 10: 1-61628-814-0

WELDON OWEN, INC.

VP, Publisher Roger Shaw
VP, Sales and Marketing Amy Kaneko
Director of Finance Phil Paulick

Associate Publisher Jennifer Newens
Associate Editor Emma Rudolph

Creative Director Kelly Booth
Art Director Alisha Petro
Senior Production Designer Rachel Lopez Metzger

Production Director Chris Hemesath
Associate Production Director Michelle Duggan

Photographer Thayer Allyson Gowdy

STUDIO
Food Stylist Erin Quon
Prop Stylist Kerrie Sherrell Walsh

LOCATION
Food Stylist Alexa Hyman
Wardrobe/Prop Stylist Jasmine Hamed
Hair/Makeup Stylist Tahni Smith/Aubri Balk Inc.
Models Stacie Overby, Robin Ayers/Look Model Agency,
Sarah Eden Davis/Look Model Agency

COVER
Food Stylist Fanny Pan
Makeup Stylist Evan Patillo

ACKNOWLEDGMENTS

Weldon Owen wishes to thank the following people for their generous support
in producing this book: Aubri Balk, Debbie Berne, Sandhya Chib, Jeffery Hasseler,
Jill Kersey, Katie Lovecraft, Lori Nunokawa, Rachael Olmstead,
Annie Rosenthal Parr, Hilary Seeley